Access and Institutional Change

Access and Institutional Change

Edited by
Oliver Fulton

The Society for Research into Higher Education
& Open University Press

Published by SRHE and
Open University Press
12 Cofferidge Close
Stony Stratford
Milton Keynes MK11 1BY

and
1900 Frost Road, Suite 101
Bristol, PA 19007, USA

First Published 1989

British Library Cataloguing in Publication Data

Access and institutional change.
  1. Great Britain. Higher education. Access
  I. Fulton, Oliver.   II. Society for Research into
  higher education
  378.41

  ISBN 0–335–09234–9 (cased)

Library of Congress catalog number is available

Typeset by Scarborough Typesetting Services
Printed in Great Britain by St Edmundsbury Press,
Bury St Edmunds, Suffolk

Contents

FULTON ?

Contributors   vii

1   Introduction   1
    Oliver Fulton

Part 1   Boundaries and Partnerships

2   Marking and Mediating the Higher-Education Boundary   7
    Gareth Parry

3   Admissions, Access and Institutional Change   29
    Oliver Fulton and Susan Ellwood

4   Access Courses   51
    John Brennan

5   Qualification, Paradigms and Experiential Learning in Higher
    Education   64
    Robin Usher

Part 2   Impact and Process

6   The Ideology of Higher Education   85
    Malcolm Tight

7   Putting Learning at the Centre of Higher Education   99
    Peter Wright

8   Access: Towards Education or Miseducation? Adults Imagine
    the Future   110
    Susan Warner Weil

Part 3   Institutional Change

9   National Policy and Institutional Development   149
    Leslie Wagner

10   Creating the Accessible Institution   163
     Chris Duke

The Society for Research into Higher Education   179

Contributors

John Brennan is Registrar for Information Services at the Council for National Academic Awards. He has written extensively about higher education and has co-authored several recent books on the relationship between higher education and the labour market.

Chris Duke has been foundation Professor and Chairman of Continuing Education at the University of Warwick, since 1985. He taught at Woolwich Polytechnic and the University of Leeds before becoming the first Director of the Centre for Continuing Education at the Australian National University 1969–85. He has extensive experience of adult and continuing education internationally, especially in the Third World.

Susan Ellwood is an administrator on the Combined Studies Programme at Lancaster Polytechnic. From April 1988 to March 1989 she was seconded to work as Research Officer at the Institute for Research and Development in Post-Compulsory Education, University of Lancaster, on a Training Agency funded research project on admissions policy and practice in higher education.

Oliver Fulton is Director of the Institute for Research and Development in Post-Compulsory Education at the University of Lancaster. His earlier academic posts were at the Universities of California (Berkeley) and Edinburgh. He has published extensively on education policy, especially in higher education.

Gareth Parry is Lecturer in Continuing Education at City University and Visiting Lecturer at the University of London, Goldsmiths' College. He was founder editor of the *Journal of Access Studies*.

Malcolm Tight is Director of the Unit for Research into Part-time Higher Education at Birkbeck College, University of London. His research interests range from the provision of, and demand for, part-time higher education, to improving our understanding of the history and philosophy of higher education as a whole.

Robin Usher is Senior Lecturer in the Adult and Post-Compulsory Education Division, School of Education, University of Southampton. He has written extensively on experiential learning, work experience and access to higher education and the theory-practice problem in adult and continuing professional education.

Leslie Wagner is Director of the Polytechnic of North London and was previously Deputy Secretary of the National Advisory Body. His earlier posts include: Head of Social Sciences at the Polytechnic of Central London and Lecturer in Economics at the Open University. He is Treasurer of the Society for Research into Higher Education.

Susan Warner Weil is Associate Director of the Higher Education for Capability Project at the RSA and Visiting Lecturer/Consultant (Adult Learning/Continuing Education) at the Centre for Higher Education Studies, Institute of Education, University of London. Her research has investigated the influences of life-long learning, and adult expectations and experiences of returning to higher education.

Peter Wright is on secondment from Portsmouth Polytechnic as a Higher Education Adviser to the Training Agency. He has taught at Sheffield and Bristol Polytechnics, the University of Leicester and the former Leeds College of Art. His field of research is the sociology of professional expertise.

1

Introduction

Oliver Fulton

Higher education is at a turning point in 1989. On the one hand, much of it looks little different from twenty years ago. If we examine it, as this book does, through the access lens (see Trow, quoted by Parry in Chapter 2, page 7) we find repeated evidence that its characteristics are still those of an 'élite' system. Full-time participation rates are little higher than in 1970; most entry criteria are still based on A levels; and in much of the system not only the curriculum and teaching methods but all the assumptions about students' backgrounds and expectations have scarcely changed. In Chapter 6 Malcolm Tight adds numerous other dimensions to this 'dominant model' or 'ideology' of élite higher education and underlines them by postulating an antithetical model which can certainly not be found within the British Isles.

On the other hand, there is now general agreement that things must change, and moderate optimism (shared by some but by no means all the contributors to this volume) that they might actually do so, or even that irreversible shifts are already taking place. The political context (also interpreted rather differently in various chapters) is certainly signalling that participation must increase substantially – perhaps even double, as Kenneth Baker first suggested in January 1989, over the next twenty-five years. Despite the very different motives, and objectives, of the mildly unholy alliance for expansion which has come into being since 1986, none of the parties involved is in any doubt that such an increase will require massive changes in institutions of higher education.

This book was specially commissioned by the Society for Research into Higher Education for its Annual Conference of 1989. And, if the historical analysis hinted at above and developed in detail by Leslie Wagner in Chapter 9 is correct, that conference's planning was peculiarly timely. Because of the change in the policy rhetoric – if not yet in the corresponding policy levers, still less in the attitudes and values expressed in the dominant model – we are at last mercifully free of the obligation to argue the case for expanded access *in principle*. Instead, we can declare that case as won – in Wagner's words, 'access is . . . legitimate, not sinful' – and move on to the far more challenging task of examining its implications.

We first learned from Martin Trow in the 1960s to distinguish between élite and mass systems of higher education, and to understand that the shift across that boundary to higher rates of participation cannot be achieved by offering 'more of the same'. If, as the optimists believe, Britain is now poised to make the leap, we need to examine more closely than ever what it is that needs to change. And our assumption here is that, whatever the role of government policy-makers or funding bodies as eggers-on, helpers or hindrances, it is changes within institutions that will make the difference. In this book we set out to define the changes that will be needed, and to speculate about the conditions under which they could occur, or are already doing so.

The book has three sections. Part 1, 'Boundaries and Partnerships', has as its focus the processes of selection for, or exclusion from, higher education. In Chapter 2 Gareth Parry takes as his organizing framework the concept of boundary and uses it to shed new light on the conventional categories which have been applied to the entry of 'non-traditional' students to higher education. In doing so he illuminates many of the confusions and conflicts – intellectual, moral, political and educational – which afflict the various 'movements' for access or accessibility.

He also, and incidentally, highlights the lack of research in this area, confirmed by Chapter 4, in which John Brennan is forced to rely on an almost hopelessly out-of-date study for his evaluation of the outcomes of Access courses. This volume was originally planned to include thorough reviews of empirical research in all the areas covered. It is no criticism of the more theoretical contributions to say that the shortage of research in such a topical area is a disappointment, and an indictment of those who should be funding it.

Chapter 3, however, is empirically based, drawing on an interview-based study of the values and practices of those directly involved in admissions to higher education, and the policy contexts in which they operate. Fulton and Ellwood present a somewhat contradictory picture, illustrating the variety of schemes and arrangements to enhance access that can be found in different parts of higher education, but also the persistence of the élite model in the conceptions and the actions of admissions tutors, and the timid and constrained responses which many of them, and their institutions, have made to the new opportunities of the 1980s. The results are fairly chastening: not only do they help to explain the resistance of many departments and institutions to increasingly plaintive calls for reform, but, by illustrating the diversity that already exists, even in a fairly tightly knit élite system, they pose troubling questions about the structure – that is, the structured inequalities – of the mass-access system that may be in prospect.

Chapters 4 and 5 look more closely at specific but key themes at the boundary. In Chapter 4 John Brennan reviews the achievements, the potential and the limitations of access courses as a bridgehead into higher education, fitting them into a typology of values about access, and complementing the broader sweep of Chapters 2 and 3; while in Chapter 5 Robin Usher takes the concept of (prior) experiential learning to ask hard questions about the different exchanges that take place across the boundary. Underlying his critique is a basic question, sobering for the optimists: namely whether formalized systems, such as mass access may well require, not only for accreditation of prior experiential learning (APEL) but for all aspects of the entry – or selection – process, are compatible with the student-centred ideology of the APEL and other access movements. In his chapter he also raises many other questions about the changing conceptions of adult abilities, of the higher-education curriculum and pedagogy, and of learning itself, which form a useful bridge to Part 2: 'Impact and Process'.

Here the emphasis shifts from admissions, selection and boundary maintenance to the internal processes of higher education, with learning itself at the core. Following Tight's introductory challenge (Chapter 6), which takes higher education's promises at their rhetorical word, asks what students might really want of it, and confronts it with the reality of what it delivers, Peter Wright, in Chapter 7, begins the process of taking learning seriously. He shows us how close are the ties between a focus on learning, or its absence, and access or accessibility for 'non-traditional' students and argues that only an institutional policy that treats learning as the central project can reconstitute higher education to meet their needs.

Chapter 8, by Susan Warner Weil, is the other contribution to this book that draws on original empirical research. In it the voices of adult learners themselves, within and outside higher education, provide us with a vivid critique of, and prescription for, their learning which is shocking in its implied indictment of what most adults experience at present. It is also sobering, for drawing on the central concept of 'disjunction' experienced by almost all her adult learner respondents, Weil concludes that neither structural change nor improved teaching and learning practices will be adequate to meet their challenge. Through all three chapters in this section runs, among others, a simple but apparently daunting theme. In Tight's words, higher education must become 'adult, not adolescent' – not just in terms of its clientele, but in its internal processes which must address and respect students as whole persons and the equals of their teachers.

Part 3 of the book is entitled 'Institutional Change'. Having spelled out some of the changes needed in the first two sections, we now address directly the problem of achieving them. It has two chapters. In the first, Leslie Wagner casts a sceptical eye on the influence of national policy, concluding that the diversity of institutions is proof in itself of the limitations of outside pressure. In the process, however, he not only provides an account of the recent history of the politics of access, but demonstrates some of the pitfalls awaiting those who wish to use financial incentives to bolster their policy rhetoric. His optimism is broadly endorsed by Chris Duke, in Chapter 10, who (after virtually demolishing any coherence the concept of access might lay claim to, and questioning the whole identity of 'institutions' of higher education) lays out a daunting list of what might constitute an accessible institution. However, with his example of Warwick University he not only illustrates the process of change in some detail, but asserts that a commitment to at least some forms of access is not necessarily incompatible with maintaining a position near the top of the status league of universities. Whether this commitment satisfies the demands of all the contributors to this volume would be an intriguing topic for research.

In a book of this kind there are omissions. As I stated at the outset, the case for widened access is assumed, not argued – though it is implicit in every contribution. More seriously, perhaps, we have not addressed some of the most crucial and unanswered policy problems – those of the macro-context within which all institutions have to operate. In particular, there is no extended discussion either of the future *system* of higher education – its structure, interconnections and control mechanisms – or the financing mechanisms to support institutions and students under a mass system. There are two defences. The first, perhaps a little cheap, is that these are the two nettles which successive governments too have proved unwilling or unable to grasp. The second, more serious, is that as Wagner argues and others confirm, national policies only facilitate, or hinder, developments which originate in institutions. It is about, and for, those working for access within those institutions that this book is written.

Part 1

Boundaries and Partnerships

2

Marking and Mediating the Higher-Education Boundary

Gareth Parry

The notion of access is popular and problematic. As a focus for discussion of policy and practice it engages with diverse issues, interests and activities external as well as internal to higher education. Yet, as a framework for analysis and action it disappoints – and often frustrates; it takes rather than makes educational problems, and confirms rather than transforms administrative and academic categories. This combination of professional engagement and theoretical closure has been a distinctive feature of contemporary access debate in relation to British higher education.

The popularity of the notion has a number of sources and dimensions. Most important perhaps has been the serviceability of the idea of 'increased' and 'wider' access: as a means of institutional survival (the numbers argument); as a source of qualified personnel (the manpower argument); as a way of extending educational opportunity (the equity argument); and as a means of changing teaching and learning in higher education (the catalyst argument). The ease with which these arguments can be related and reconciled in numerous policy statements is a measure of the adaptability and versatility of the access idea (Council for Industry and Higher Education 1987; National Advisory Body 1988; Royal Society of Arts 1988). Indeed, access awareness has assumed populist proportions across and beyond the educational arena.

The attractiveness of the notion of access for synoptic and comparative purposes has received less attention, and the potential of this perspective has only just begun to be examined and explored in the British context.

There are hardly any issues in higher education that cannot be approached through the perspective of access, and in a way that has the advantage of showing the links and connections among different elements of higher educational system.

(Trow 1981)

Notwithstanding its obvious currency and evident suggestiveness, the analytical and critical value of the notion has been seen to be in some doubt.

The public platform offered to policy-makers and practitioners to debate the access question has exposed serious shortcomings in the nature of access discourse and development. This has been particularly apparent at the level of the institution where the invitation to reflect on experience, plan for change and identify a strategy has rarely moved the access debate beyond the familiar and anecdotal. As an exercise in professional dialogue and review there is much here to confirm Tolley's (1980) early observation that discussion of access to higher education 'quickly leads to a parade of hobby horses, of vested interests and of prejudices'.

For Griffin, this dominance of the institutional significance of access in professional discourse and practice is a measure of the 'ideological function' of the concept which has 'provision' rather than 'curriculum' as its object.

> For the problem of access is seen primarily in terms of the access of individuals (either as such or else as members of particular groups) to learning opportunities, the barriers to which are constituted in wholly material terms. In fact barriers to access are collectively as much as individually experienced and culturally as well as materially constructed, and the paradox lies in confronting the individual learner with the problem of the socially and culturally constructed contents of learning. All the barriers likely to be experienced in these circumstances are equally real, but access does seem to be conceptualized in terms which ignore the cultural barriers, which isolate and abstract the individual learner, and which tend to reduce the issue to one wholly resolvable in technical and institutional terms. There is little sense here that access to education might be a collective and political issue of knowledge and power in society.
>
> (Griffin 1983)

Put another way, the theoretical potential of the idea of 'access' – access to the (problematic) structures of knowledge embodied in the curriculum – is rendered or reduced to the narrower notion of 'accessibility': a conception conveyed in the language of openness, flexibility and transferability. In this more familiar and received form, institutional barriers to change 'rather than the social dynamics of change and cultural resistances' (ibid.) become the objects of policy and strategy; and educational innovation is made possible without disturbing traditional curriculum categories and contents. Access, along with needs and provision, constitute a professional ideology which operates to 'depoliticize' curriculum questions and to pre-empt critical analysis. Within this ideological trinity the significance of access is distinctive and pervasive:

> the ideological content of access is constructed by the professional need to impute learning needs to greater numbers of people. Access

is a need of the system itself, in other words, and in this respect it is similarly conceptualized in higher and further education.

(ibid.)

Griffin identified the professional ideology of access, needs and practices with the field of 'adult education', but his analysis has direct relevance to the discussion of what has become known as the 'access movement' spanning further, higher and adult education.

The major perspectives, principles and practices associated with this 'movement' (or, more accurately, movements and tendencies) are the subject of this paper. The intention here is not to begin a theoretical critique of access ideology and practice; nor is it to provide a comprehensive and detailed survey of access arrangements. What will be attempted is more modest and tentative: a discursive mapping of the main contours and features of access routes and relationships as they relate to the entry of adults to higher education at undergraduate level. The focus on adults – especially those not holding formal or conventional qualifications ('non-traditional students') – and undergraduate entry will be justified in terms of the significance which these two categories have for an élite system of higher education and its anticipated movement in the direction of a 'mass' model.

Policy contexts and episodes

The overdetermination of the access notion and the undertheorization of the access field have already been suggested as reasons for the problematic nature of access discourse. There are other and related reasons which derive more from the nature of the political and educational context in which competing access strategies have been proposed.

Like a number of other departures from traditional codes and practices, the recent growth of interest and investment in access experiment illustrates the paradox of 'innovation through recession' (Squires 1983). It coincided with the onset of retrenchment in higher education in the late 1970s and followed a period of demand-led expansion based on the willingness of growing numbers of 'qualified' students to enter the academy. With the exception (and possibly because) of the establishment of the Open University, there had been few attempts to stimulate demand above and beyond the 'qualified' pool. Government policy had instead been limited to 'the passive underwriting of student places' (Neave 1985).

The failure of British higher education in the 1970s to move beyond its élite phase of development (Neave 1982a) and its subsequent 'regressive' phase in the 1980s (Neave 1985) provided the background against which a range of arguments about increased participation and wider access were launched and advanced. The 'defensiveness' of these early arguments and agendas reflected the prevailing mood and harsh climate (Fulton 1981).

However, the policy themes of this period – moderate demand, stringent selection and maintained standards (Department of Education and Science 1985b) – have since given way to promises of improvement in the level and pattern of participation. Maximum participation, responsible admission and raised standards (Department of Education and Science 1987) now define the policy priorities for a system which will attack demographic decline through a process of substitution (fewer conventional students replaced by more non-traditional entrants) rather than an expansion of student numbers.

The projections for the 1990s envisage an increase in the proportions of young people and adults achieving entry to higher education, and a full-time participation index of around eighteen per cent (compared with the current fourteen per cent) by the end of the century. The possibility of a breakthrough to mass higher education in the terms outlined by Trow (1974) has, understandably, given a new impetus to the search for access 'solutions' and a new confidence to practitioners in their pursuit of access 'alternatives'. At the same time, the new enthusiasm for wider access and the rediscovery of the adult student have enabled the government to seize the access initiative and to recover much of the ground – tactical and ideological – ceded to erstwhile advocates and adversaries.

The cooling-out and delegitimation of particular access activities in the early and middle parts of the decade and their selective warming-up and affirmation in the recent period is well illustrated by the contrasting policy treatment of two Department-of-Education-and-Science-supported initiatives which have survived the passage from the margin to the mainstream of educational thinking. Both experienced low-key origins and high-profile destinations, but their separate journeys help to explain the disjointed features of the contemporary access environment. Furthermore, their early encounters with proponents and critics of flexible learning and positive action serve to remind us of the well-rehearsed, sometimes overrehearsed, quality of current exchanges.

One initiative began as an invitation to national bodies in 1975 to consider the establishment of national arrangements for credit transfer in further and higher education. The other was an invitation to selected local authorities in 1978 to consider setting up 'special' preparatory courses for adults, to assist ethnic minority groups in particular to qualify for training in teaching, social work and similar professions. A feasibility study into the need for a national information service on credit transfer and an evaluation study of 'access studies to higher education' were commissioned by the Department of Education and Science and their recommendations, each supporting the extension of their respective initiatives, were presented to government in due course (Toyne 1979; Millins 1984).

The response to the Toyne report was, first, authorization for a regional pilot scheme and then approval in 1982 for a national educational counselling and credit-transfer information service (ECCTIS). This new service would 'provide information about actual entry requirements for courses and about the credit that may be granted for previous studies' and, with the wider development of modular courses and credit transfer, would help 'students to build on their studies progressively and to mix full-time and part-time study' (Department of Education and Science 1985b). This support in the Green Paper on higher education was widened and strengthened in the following White Paper: national and regional credit-transfer schemes now 'help to extend higher education opportunities' to a 'wider range of entrants'; academic credit can be sought for 'prior learning, whether gained through formal qualifications or experience'; and students will increasingly be able to pursue programmes of study 'tailored to their particular needs but within established academic standards' (Department of Education and Science 1987).

The response to the Millins report and its conference reminder (Millins, Reyersbach and Yates 1985) was indirect. The research was unacknowledged, and the reply came care of a government committee of inquiry on academic validation in public-sector higher education:

> as regards access courses intended to prepare for entry to degree courses students lacking the minimum entry qualifications normally required, we believe that institutions should bear in mind the possible dangers in themselves organizing or helping to organize such courses with a view to admitting students from them to their own degree courses. Arrangements of this kind can result in the formation of relationships and understandings which lead to students from the access courses being accepted for degree courses even if they lack the ability to reach degree standard. Institutions must avoid giving access course students any reason to suppose that they are automatically assured of places on degree courses. As a general principle, an access course should not be designed with a specific institution or course in mind, but should seek recognition from several institutions as being a suitable preparation for their courses. . . .
>
> . . . we wish to emphasize that institutions should not accept too high a proportion of mature students and/or students lacking the normal minimum entry qualifications for degree courses which are not specifically designed for them. Such students can be very able, but often lack the technical skills of studying needed for effective study at degree level. Different approaches are needed for different types of student. If too high a proportion of students is accepted for courses not designed for them they may founder and staff may be tempted to lower standards.
>
> (Department of Education and Science 1985a)

The impact of these prescriptions, although abbreviated and tempered in the Green Paper of the same year (Department of Education and Science 1985b), was to mobilize practitioners and others in defence of the access-course idea and in support of collaborative access arrangements targeted at disadvantaged and underrepresented groups. At the same time, demographic prospects and manpower requirements appear to have provoked a revaluation. In a significant policy shift the later White Paper elevated Access courses to a designation as one of the three 'generally recognized' routes into higher education (alongside traditional sixth-form qualifications and vocational qualifications), and promised their future development with a 'comprehensive framework' for recognition and validation. Access courses designed to offer entry to more than one institution were to be preferred 'wherever practicable', but government did now accept the place of those geared to a particular receiving institution 'provided that effective oversight is exercised by the appropriate validating authority' (Department of Education and Science 1987). A more detailed discussion of Access courses and an account of political responses to them are given by John Brennan in Chapter 4.

Access dimensions and directions

These two episodes indicate something of the inconsistency of recent government policy on higher education but, more particularly, they point to characteristic features of the contemporary access scene: its competing conceptions; its dynamism and diversity; its narrow empirical and research base; and its focus on learners and learning.

The first of these features has been the most conspicuous and widely commented upon (Duke 1986; Tight forthcoming). In the absence of a comprehensive policy, different access philosophies have been identified with different types and levels of access initiative. The policy directions already sketched have assisted this process, as have alternative and countervailing policies at local and institutional level. What were seen as complementary approaches and arrangements have become more polarized positions at opposite ends of an access continuum.

At one end can be located a cluster of arguments in support of a more coherent and accessible 'system' encompassing all forms of postcompulsory learning and embracing education and training opportunities in all sectors (Unit for the Development of Adult Continuing Education 1988); a wide-ranging concept of access in which the recognition of prior learning and the accumulation and transfer of credit combine to change the balance of power between individual learners and educational institutions (Evans 1985). At the other end can be found more strategic and situated interpretations of the access project based on designated courses, targeted audiences, selected sectors, consecutive stages, specified routes and guaranteed places (Further Education Unit 1987a); or a perception of the 'Access course' as a key agent of change on behalf of underrepresented groups in higher education (Woodrow 1988).

At the same time, the tension between access in the general and access in the particular should not be overinterpreted. Both accommodate competing ideologies and interests, and both operate in parallel to expose and eliminate 'barriers' to learning, whether they be financial, institutional, structural, situational, geographical, educational, informational or attitudinal (Advisory Council for Adult and Continuing Education 1982). Moreover, the division is less evident on the ground where access arrangements display a wide variety of forms and combinations (Michaels 1986).

As to the second feature, what were still pioneering and singular developments in the early 1980s (Percy 1985) have become part of more plural and diversified systems in the late 1980s. Principles of collaboration and partnership have underpinned much of this expansion: across departments and faculties as part of associate-student schemes (Slowey 1988); between further- and higher-education institutions in the case of many Access courses (Parry 1986); across adult-, further- and higher-education sectors in respect of open colleges and access federations (Browning 1986); and across education, training and employment in relation to regional consortia for credit transfer. As before, the pattern of development has been uneven and varied, reflecting institutional profiles and priorities as well as local circumstances. Most such initiatives have emerged 'from below' and reflect local-authority interest in post-school education.

Thirdly, the recency of many access arrangements and the opacity of most admission procedures have made for a meagre research base and literature. Apart from studies of participation and performance (Brennan 1986; Bourner and Hamed 1987; Davies and Yates 1987; Woodley *et al.* 1987), occasional surveys of access programmes and procedures (Evans 1984; Lucas and Ward 1985) and some evaluation studies of early schemes (Percy, Powell and Flude 1983; Inner London Education Authority 1984; Smithers and Griffin 1986), there has been little opportunity to appraise policy and compare practice in a systematic manner. The forthcoming reports of a number of access-related projects by the CNAA Development Fund should increase the empirical coverage, as will extension of ECCTIS to include Access courses.

Even the identification of the non-traditional or 'non-standard' entrant – the priority group for most access initiatives – has proved difficult, given the residual category of 'other' qualifications in official statistics. However, a recent DES Statistical Bulletin has attempted a partial disaggregation of this category for mature students entering higher education in the academic year beginning 1986. It is reported below both as an indication of the technical problems and as a reminder of the scale of the access 'problem'.

In the *polytechnics and colleges* sector, which accounts for over eighty per cent of mature entrants and where most students are on sub-degree courses, over a quarter of all [*full-time*] first degree entrants aged 25 or over are exceptional admissions or have no known qualifications, but less than 10 per cent of those aged 21–24 falls into this category. The

remaining *full-time* students have a variety of other qualifications on
entry ranging from degrees and professional qualifications to GCE
O-level or City and Guilds qualifications. . . . Less than 12 per cent of
part-time first degree students in polytechnics and colleges have
traditional qualifications on entry but almost half of those aged 21–24
have BTEC or equivalent qualifications. 'Other' qualifications account
for 28 per cent of those aged 21–24 and 70 per cent of those aged 25 or
more. [Among these,] less than 10 per cent of those aged 21–24 and
just over a quarter of those aged 25 or more were exceptional
admissions or had no known qualifications. The rest had a variety of
other qualifications, degrees, teacher training qualifications (for the
older students), professional qualifications and GCE O-levels.

In the *universities*, half of all *full-time* mature students have other UK
qualifications, and half have no qualifications. [My emphasis]
                    (Department of Education and Science 1988)

With the benefit of this breakdown, it is easier to confirm earlier estimates
of the proportion of full-time 'non-standard' entrants as 'well under ten per
cent across the system as a whole' (Fulton 1988).

The final general feature of the access enterprise has been a concern with
adults as learners, and the ways in which learning acquired through prior
experience, previous education and training, or access and other studies
could or should relate to learning in higher education. The question of
could or should has been a central and critical theme. For example, the
application of portfolio assessment and similar procedures to identify
appropriate learning derived from experience and the use of Access
courses to prepare adults for the demands of undergraduate study have
been able to demonstrate some success in progressing non-traditional
students into higher education. Their experimental period may now be
claimed to be over, except perhaps in relation to more linear and
knowledge-based disciplines. But the struggle to convince external agencies of the validity and reliability of these arrangements has served to
sharpen debate within the access community about the kind of relationship
to be formed with higher education. In more concrete terms, it has posed
the question whether such arrangements should seek to match prior
learning or to tie preparatory study to the course requirements and
regimes of mainstream higher education. A close correspondence with
higher education may secure access and progression, but the need for
parallel change in higher education may be delayed or denied, reducing
the potential for innovation in the access process. The exercise of
specifying the learning outcomes to be used as a basis for alternative entry
to higher education has been, in many cases, a novel and illuminating
experience. It has involved more than a simple exchange between those
within and without higher education. More significant has been the search
for a common language to mediate the different conceptions of education
and learning brought into play: on the one side a subject-based approach

referenced to A-level formulas and requirements, and on the other a learner-centred perspective suited to individual needs, interests and requirements. In this situation, the onus has been on higher education to make available the criteria to be applied in judging 'ability to benefit' and to make explicit the curriculum principles and learning goals to which these criteria relate.

The difficulties, uncertainties and sensitivities exposed by access encounters of this kind have highlighted the importance of boundary management and control. An élite system of higher education has required the maintenance of a strong boundary between itself and other sources of learning in order to protect the qualities invested in a 'higher' education. That boundary has reinforced a notion of discontinuity and distance from other forms of learning, yet arrangements for crossing the boundary have assumed continuity and articulation. The tensions and ambiguities which accompany this paradox may be observed in relation to the way alternative access arrangements for non-traditional students are conducted and negotiated at the boundary. Stripped of the screen and the convenience of the A-level 'standard' and the buffer of the formal examination and entry system, the boundary becomes much more vulnerable to ideas which probe the tacit nature of much of higher education.

The concept of boundary has been popular in academic commentaries on the state of higher education (Neave 1982b; Schuller, Tight and Weil 1988). Its advantage for the present discussion is that it directs attention to the location of access arrangements and the different forms of engagement with higher education which they presuppose. Furthermore an examination of the boundary–access nexus will help to indicate the scope of current access activity and the capacity of existing access models to accelerate the movement to a more open and broadly based system of mass higher education. With these aims in mind, a distinction will be drawn between access procedures which operate on the boundary, access programmes which stand outside the boundary, and access arrangements which mediate the boundary. Although the categories overlap and interlock, they have developed as discrete and sometimes competing approaches, each with their own ideologies and practices fashioned to 'new' constituencies of adult students.

On the boundary

Given the dominance of a full-time higher-education system directed at qualified school leavers, open and direct entry to part-time higher education has been an accessible and popular route into first-degree study for mature and non-traditional students. The majority of this part-time adult undergraduate population has been enrolled at the Open University 'whose own particular solution to the access problem was to do away with entry qualifications' (Woodley 1987). Subject to ability to pay, admission has been on a first-come, first-served basis and foundation courses in all subject fields have been designed so that they can be studied by adults with little prior knowledge. However, those not holding 'normal' higher-education qualifications have comprised a minority of applicants, and those with 'low' qualifications have been more likely to withdraw and have been less successful in the first year of study. Again, although their performance has grown no worse in relation to that of the highly qualified in recent years, 'when it comes to graduation it seems that the gap is big and growing' (ibid.). Tight has summarized the problem in the following terms:

> Open entry, while reducing the question of access to one of resources – i.e. first come, first served – introduces other problems. There is a risk of very high levels of student attrition if adequate preparatory provision, covering both generic study skills and subject specific knowledge, is not made available. The Open University has only recently begun to get to grips with this problem . . . having previously abdicated the provision of preparatory courses to public, voluntary and private sector institutions.
>
> (Tight 1987)

The pattern of entry to part-time higher education in the polytechnics and colleges – the other major providers – is different. Although seven out of eight first-degree mature students were not in possession of the traditional entry qualifications for higher education, a large number of them (nearly half of younger adults) held BTEC or equivalent qualifications – reflecting the subject balance of courses in the sector. The recognition of vocational qualifications and experience appears to have encouraged providers of part-time degree courses to be more flexible and sensitive in their access arrangements: an expectation 'borne out to an increasing extent in practice, but not in a uniform fashion' (ibid.).

As Evans has noted, the application of direct or special entry procedures is likely to be most positive where adults are the target or normal audience for higher education.

> The clearest evidence that applicants' needs are the highest priority is usually found where courses have either been designed with older students in mind, or where large numbers of older students have populated the course for some time. There, admissions procedures are seen as the beginning of a continuous service to older students which gives them support, encouragement and advice right through to the end of their course.
>
> (Evans 1984)

If so, the adult orientation of part-time higher education is not simply a reflection of the increased and more flexible access made available to those unable or unwilling to study full time, but becomes an expression of an intrinsic quality or value, creating an appropriate environment for innovation and experiment. According to Tight (1987), there is, or should be, 'something about higher education, or perhaps the highest education, which is peculiarly adult and, consequently, particularly valuable and pre-disposed towards being organized on something other than a full-time basis'. Developments such as modularization, credit transfer and independent study 'have been more prevalent in part-time provision, and are more relevant to it because of its essentially adult orientation' (ibid.).

The permeability of the higher-education boundary for the part-time degree or associate student is in contrast to the degree of boundary control and closure exercised in relation to the full-time entrant. Clearly, the strength of the boundary will vary by sector, institution and subject, but the authority and priority accorded to traditional sixth-form qualifications has limited opportunities for direct entry to full-time courses by 'unqualified' adults. The reluctance of polytechnics and colleges to admit non-standard entrants was attributed by Evans (1984) to two main features: the influence of a CNAA mythology relating to a ten-per-cent limit on non-standard entrants; and the inadequacy of the techniques and procedures to assess individuals as potential students. In the case of the first, a revision of CNAA regulations has countered this tendency, but a similar set of messages may now be heard in respect of certain of the professional bodies. (See Fulton and Ellwood, Chapter 3 of this volume, for a further account of the inhibiting factors in universities, polytechnics and colleges.) Less progress would appear to have been made in the case of the second where conceptual as well as practical difficulties have delayed the introduction of the assessment of prior learning into the admissions process (Usher 1986 and Chapter 5 of this volume).

The reluctance of the universities to invest in adult and non-traditional students has been more conspicuous and their early response to direct entry was to establish a limited number of 'special' admission procedures for mature entry (Jones and Williams 1979). The largest and best-known – the JMB mature-entry scheme operated on behalf of five northern universities – has been the subject of a detailed evaluation study (Smithers and Griffin 1986). The procedure comprises an application form, a formal interview and a series of 'unseen and uncircumscribed' examination papers; in other words, a proxy for GCE A-level but without the benefit of a set syllabus or past papers. Unsurprisingly, nearly two-thirds of applicants did not matriculate and those that did performed on average better than other university students, especially in areas 'where experience plays an important part'. Although other universities have less formal and more diversified arrangements, the need to identify with the A-level style and 'standard' has been a common and continuing concern.

Direct entry or special admission by individual application is the form of alternative entry procedure which has the longest history. Access arrangements of this kind operate on the higher-education boundary and, along with the open entry procedures of the Open University, they mark one side – the inside – of it. Operationally, they have similar strengths and weaknesses. Both open and special admission systems should offer direct entry, with credit recognition or advanced standing as appropriate, to adults who are able to demonstrate their ability to benefit in a valid and reliable way. For these applicants, there should be no ritual requirement to enter into preliminary rites of passage, such as access or preparatory courses, to secure their place in the system. However, one of the limiting factors bearing on direct entry for both tutor and applicant has been the inadequacy or indeterminacy of procedures to demonstrate and assess prior learning. The admission tutor's responsibility for conducting these activities or evaluating their results has not been clear. Direct entry for non-traditional students should imply diversifying the role of the tutor to embrace advice, counselling and referral as well as assessment and selection. At present, however, as Fulton and Ellwood show in Chapter 3, it is the selective rather than the service function which prevails.

The assessment and evaluation of previous experience should have a particular importance for non-traditional learners:

> it is a most important facility for the less confident potential student, those less aware of the value of their prior experience, and those less able to articulate and demonstrate orally, in writing or in other ways the state of readiness for higher education which previous aspects of their life have given them. . . . [But] . . . we need to ensure that such a route is in fact a facility for those who need it, and does not come to be seen by institutions of higher education as a requirement and a barrier to prospective students who might be able to present themselves for special admission without engaging in an intermediate process of this kind. . . . [In practice] to be able to take advantage of it the student first needs to know that the opportunity exists for special admission, needs confidence and ability to manage her or his progress through institutional admission systems, and needs a capacity for articulating the case that can be made.
>
> (Gibson 1986)

Beyond the boundary

The location of these procedures on the boundary of a selective competitive and school-orientated system of higher education has made it difficult for admissions tutors to acquire an understanding of the learning environments for adults outside the boundary. The access and preparatory programmes which inhabit this latter territory have generally identified with the liberal tradition of adult education and have sought to sustain student-centred and informal styles of learning in contradistinction to the discipline-led pedagogy of higher education and the credentialism and vocationalism of further education. Their distance from higher education – structural, cultural and ideological – and their cultivation of a separate and autonomous tradition have helped to mark the other side – the outside – of the higher-education boundary.

Unlike the entrant tackling special admission procedures in search of a particular course at a particular institution, the applicant from this kind of programme will usually apply for entry in the same way as the conventionally qualified school-leaver. Intending students will then rely on their designation as 'mature applicants' and their personal statements and references to secure an interview and the offer of a place. Sometimes an adult may pursue both special-admission and normal entry routes, but this seems to be uncommon. Sometimes applicants or their tutors will make informal contact with an admissions tutor in advance of a formal application, but in most cases the application will be dealt with in the normal way. However, the disadvantage enjoined by normal entry arrangements may well be reduced where the applicant is sponsored by a long-established and well-regarded course.

The majority of courses are part time, local and supported by local authorities and the responsible bodies (see Chapter 4 for a fuller description). They are described by a variety of titles, although 'fresh start' has emerged as a generic term to cover most courses. Openness, discovery and opportunity appear to be guiding principles and access to higher education may or may not be a primary orientation. In the case of Fresh Horizons courses pioneered at the City Literary Institute since the 1960s, they were

> never conceived only as 'access' opportunities to higher education. They were intended to be valid in their own right: they are best defined as 'developmental', allowing for self-discovery and growth and for decision-making on future aims and objectives as growth takes place.
> (Hutchinson and Hutchinson 1986)

The open-entry and open-exit philosophy serves to distinguish them from other types of access provision in adult and further education as well as to explain in part their attractiveness to women and their basis in the humanities and social sciences. Students may enrol initially with or without a higher-education target. Many of the early courses were established in institutes of adult education where the process of returning to study was often more important than preparation for particular forms of education, training or employment. The introduction of these courses into university adult education has tended to strengthen their access dimension, but their association with a university has not in the main compromised their open-endedness: relationships with other departments of the university have remained indirect and informal, and the parent university has usually been only one of a number of destinations for students. Indeed, they represent a healthy reaction against the narrow and specialist subject-based programmes of much of traditional extra-mural and WEA education (Jones and Johnson 1983).

Another access route within the liberal tradition – extended in length and exceptional in mode – has been the long-term adult residential colleges such as Ruskin, Northern, Fircroft and Hillcroft which provide one-year and two-year full-time courses for resident students, 'the vast majority of whom left school at sixteen with few educational qualifications' (Lieven 1987). Their high unit costs and the limited numbers they enrol have recently led to a diversification of their work and more collaboration with local providers. At the same time, an increased focus on access to higher education is seen as offering

> a more instrumental and problematic role for the institution preparing students for a system not noted for its responsiveness to the needs, values and aspirations of working class people. A curriculum defined solely in the context of a college can focus on the interests, needs and methods appropriate to the constituency of that college. Once entry into higher education becomes an explicit and primary aim, then a training in the rituals and differentiating hurdles of higher education becomes an essential and defining component of the college curriculum. The process might be very good at getting people into higher education, but it does not look like much of an alternative, radical or otherwise.
>
> (ibid.)

Near the boundary

A similar concern about the capacity of higher education to influence and distort curricula in other parts of post-school education has informed the development of open-college networks and federations: local and regional arrangements designed to bring together areas of provision in adult, further and higher education previously separated by structure and ideology. The first of these open-college federations, the Open College of the North-West, involves part-time courses for adults taught in local adult- and further-education colleges and centres and based on syllabuses agreed and validated by two institutions of higher education. Adults can enrol for courses at two levels: Stage A which is introductory and Stage B which is 'preparatory'. Passes at Stage B with certain grades are recognized by the two validators and other institutions as achieving the general matriculation requirement for entry to higher education. Although established as the 'Alternatives to A-level Scheme' and with access to higher education very much in mind

> few students on Open College courses have deliberate and unequivocal notions of preparation for higher education, of moving through several Stage A and two Stage B units towards entry to higher education. Rather the pattern is for adults, once over the initial confidence hurdle, to do their own thing, to use Open College courses

to fit their own intrinsic, and often short-term study and life-plans and, perhaps, to move on to other course provision or forms of study.

(Percy 1988)

In recognition of the different sources and trajectories of adult and lifelong learning, an alternative model of open-college collaboration has developed, based on the accreditation of courses and activities at a number of levels from basic education to entry to higher education. The model is well illustrated by the Manchester Open College Federation (MOCF) which accredits courses at four levels. Course recognition is conducted by panels composed of tutors submitting courses for recognition and advisers drawn from appropriate educational institutions. Credits are awarded to students on the recommendation of the course tutor and subject to independent moderation. Although organized around a 'linear core', the framework is designed to facilitate 'lateral' movement to militate against 'new structures through which people must pass, corridor-like, to destinations which educators suggest and control (Browning 1986).

Within the federation open-exit access courses are seen to benefit from a form of accreditation which creates space for innovative teaching and learning and which offers students a 'passport' to the higher-education institutions to which they apply.

It is the provider who designs courses to be validated by the MOCF. This alteration in focus has wide implications, retaining and underpinning as it does, the local autonomy of individual courses. This has the advantage that what is 'guaranteed' by the MOCF is not that students have acquired a certain body of knowledge influenced by a pre-determined exit, but that they have studied an approved teacher-designed body of knowledge at a particular mutually agreed level.

(Kearney and Diamond 1987: 38)

Open-college collaboration, validation and accreditation may seem far removed from the negotiated curricula of fresh-start programmes but, in terms of access routes, processes and outcomes, they share similar features of openness, flexibility and choice. On the other hand, they display different degrees of autonomy from higher education and exercise different degrees of leverage on the admissions process. Open-college arrangements invite more involvement from higher education and in return the portability of their course validation or accreditation is increased across higher education. In terms of mature admission, this may extend to a policy of 'favourable consideration' or 'guaranteed interview'; an advance on 'eligibility', yet expressed in a passive rather than an active voice. To achieve a more positive stance has usually required a more formal coupling of the access parties.

Through the boundary

Access arrangements which promote a direct and dynamic engagement with higher education may be seen to mediate the boundary in ways which enable higher education institutions and departments to commit places to prospective students in advance of applications. In other words, to establish 'negotiated and guaranteed progression procedures on to specified courses at particular HE institutions' (Further Education Unit 1987a). The argument for formal undertakings and relationships of this kind has rested on a number of claims: some of which have a basis in available evidence and others which have yet to be tested.

Underlying these has been the relative failure of existing access arrangements to increase the participation of adults not holding formal qualifications and thereby to challenge the underrepresentation of

> those groups who have been least well-served by the school system and who face particular barriers to entry to higher education. These include ethnic minorities, especially the black communities; women, especially those who, through early parenthood or the need to work, had to abandon their education; and working class adults, especially the unemployed, whose talents may not have been fully recognized at the secondary stage.
>
> (ibid.)

Hence, it is claimed, for those groups to have confidence in alternative access arrangements there needs to be a 'contract' entered into by all three parties – student, access provider and receiving institution – which can 'guarantee' entry to a specified course in higher education, based on successful completion of an approved programme of study.

Although special admission procedures for individual applicants might be thought to have the same potential, their ability to reach disadvantaged and disaffected groups has been in doubt. This has been one reason why full-time rather than part-time higher education has been the object of most linked-access schemes. Indeed, underneath the argument for targeted and guaranteed access arrangements has been a determination to avoid the marginalization of adults in sub-degree and part-time courses and to resist 'the trend, common in adult education, of provision specifically designed for systemically disadvantaged groups being rapidly appropriated by people who already have educational advantages' (Lieven 1988).

A second and related claim has to do with quality and control. The involvement of higher education in the design, delivery and management of access programmes has been justified in terms of the 'careful balance' to be achieved between the learning needs of returning adults and the threshold requirements of higher-education courses: 'It must not be so weighted towards a student-centred approach as to fail to prepare students for a higher education environment, nor so content-laden as to become indistinguishable from an "A" level syllabus' (Woodrow 1988). Further-more, the possibility of extending access opportunities to mathematics-based and science-based higher education – a no-go area for many older students – has been claimed to depend on a depth and intensity of carefully planned preparation which recognizes the limited scope for broadening and compensating study in the first year of degree courses in such discipline areas.

Finally, and in some tension with the previous claim, there is the expectation that communication between access partners and with access entrants will begin to change attitudes, policies and practices inside higher education. Woodrow has identified three stages in this change process: the actual decision by a higher-education institution to become involved in an access initiative, 'a recognition, however hesitant, that non-traditional students would be acceptable'; the negotiation of an appropriate curricu-lum with external providers and agencies, 'itself a valuable staff develop-ment process'; and the direct experience of teaching access students and access entrants, 'probably the greatest influence for change' (ibid.).

The major vehicle for this form of boundary mediation has been the linked Access course which combines the principles of targeting, collabora-tion and progression. The recent exponential growth of such courses has contributed to a further diversification of modes, subjects, relationships and models. Even so, such schemes remain largely a feature of the further-education scene and mainly a bottom-up development: often initiated by individuals at section and departmental level, supported to different degrees by local authorities, and in some cases enhanced by open-college relationships and encouraged by regional and national planning bodies.

Linked Access courses usually operate as discrete programmes offering part-time or full-time preparation for one or more courses, at one or more levels, in one or more institutions of higher education. The early single-outlet model has given way to more multilateral relationships which aim to progress students to a number of linked courses in a similar subject field. Again, the early emphasis on education, social work, social science and humanities has been reduced somewhat by new courses which relate to more vocational and science-based subjects (Osborne 1988), and the universities – through in-house as well as linked courses – have begun to share in this development (Parry 1989). Finally, although identified initially with improved access for ethnic minority groups, most schemes target all categories of non-traditional entrant. However, they have continued to prove particularly attractive and effective for black-minority adults (Inner London Education Authority 1984; Further Education Unit 1987b; Ball 1988; Lyon 1988) and there has been little evidence of the emergent ghettoization which was feared by some (Williams *et al.* 1988).

Unlike more open-ended access programmes, linked Access courses provide a rapid and intensive preparation for those students who have already identified a wish to enter higher education and who have particular courses in mind. Moreover, they often require applicants to demonstrate at entry their potential to complete the course successfully. The consequent constraints on openness and flexibility in many destination-led schemes have contributed to the adoption of multilateral models as well as open-entry 'planning periods' which precede 'main programmes' customized to individual students (Pelissier and Smith 1988). This tension between openness and negotiation on the one hand and collaboration and progression on the other has been a source of innovation as well as friction within the wider access movement.

Prospects and possibilities

The significance of contemporary access arrangements for the survival or otherwise of an élite form of higher education may be observed and investigated at the edge of the system. The strength, stability and clarity of this boundary – properties characteristic of the British system – have been questioned at different points and to various degrees by alternative access routes and relationships which anticipate new audiences and broader purposes for a 'higher' education. In broad terms, they may be said to have disturbed rather than challenged the separateness and exclusiveness of higher education. Nevertheless, their different alignments suggest other possibilities.

For Trow, the only prospect of a movement to a mass system of continuing higher education in Britain will depend on a closer association with further education, a set of institutions 'very little spoken of by educators and almost never by academics' and 'which might be the instrument for the provision of post-secondary education to really large proportions of the adult population' (Trow 1987). The major thrust of recent access activity has been in this direction, both in the establishment of access courses which begin to articulate the two sectors and in the formation of open colleges and regional consortia which promote their association. In a more recent paper, Trow has referred to these and similar developments as 'the accumulation of small deviations' from the accepted norms and patterns of British higher education, indicating that the system is 'becoming more diverse in response to myriad uncoordinated decisions by different institutions and academic units' (Trow 1989).

Most observers would recognize the restricted, uncoordinated and uneven nature of these developments. In their separate attempts to build more open provision and alternative pathways, new identities have been created, new boundaries formed and new hierarchies established. The self-sufficiency of open-access systems (such as the Open University) and the self-containment of special admission procedures have worked against more local forms of collaboration, while the new regard for access courses directed specifically at higher education has tended to increase stratification as well as segmentation in the access landscape; a process which may be reinforced by the establishment of a national framework for the recognition of access courses (Council for National Academic Awards 1989) and which may bring more regulation and restriction of access activity.

One consequence of the application of this framework will be to focus public and professional attention on the strategic role of further education in increasing demand for and access to higher education. Unlike the school and adult-education sectors, further education has been open to both younger and older students and has been identified with each of the 'generally recognized' routes into higher education: 'conventional access' through A-level and GCSE examinations in a variety of subjects; 'staged access' to vocational higher education through BTEC and other qualifications at intermediate and higher levels; and 'accelerated access' through subject-related Access courses linked to local institutions of higher education. Moreover, two of these routes have been significant for groups which continue to be underrepresented in higher education: the vocational route for working-class entrants and the Access-course route for black-minority students.

A closer alignment of further education and higher education in these terms would appear to be a tidy and safe solution, requiring colleges to strengthen and coordinate their provision along these three fronts and addressing within a common institutional framework the 'numbers', 'manpower' and 'equity' arguments alluded to at the beginning of this chapter. It would also be a limited solution, leaving the curriculum categories and processes of higher education largely untouched and relying on student-centred access programmes to win continued legitimacy for subject-loaded degree environments – the boundary mediated, even permeated, but yet to be transformed.

References

Advisory Council for Adult and Continuing Education (1982) *Continuing Education: From Policies to Practice*, Leicester, Advisory Council for Adult and Continuing Education.

Ball, W. (1988) 'Equal opportunities and post-sixteen education: strategies for institutional change, possibilities and constraints', *Journal of Further and Higher Education*, 12 (1), 54–69.

Bourner, T. and Hamed, M. (1987) 'Degree awards in the public sector of higher education: comparative results for A-level entrants and non-A-level entrants', *Journal of Access Studies*, 2 (1), 25–41.

Brennan, J. (1986) 'Student learning and the "capacity to benefit": the performance of non-traditional students in public sector higher education', *Journal of Access Studies*, 1 (2), 23–32.

Browning, D. (1986) 'Access to what . . . and for whom?', *Education for Capability Newsletter* (spring).

Council for Industry and Higher Education (1987) *Towards a Partnership*, London, Council for Industry and Higher Education.

Council for National Academic Awards (1989) *Access Courses to Higher Education: A Framework of National Arrangements for Recognition*, London, Council for National Academic Awards.

Davies, P. and Yates, J. (1987) 'The progress of former Access students in higher education', *Journal of Access Studies*, 2 (1), 7–11.

Department of Education and Science (1985a) *Academic Validation in Public Sector Higher Education: the Report of the Committee of Enquiry into the Academic Validation of Degree Courses in Public Sector Higher Education*, Cmnd 9501, London, HMSO.

Department of Education and Science (1985b) *The Development of Higher Education into the 1990s*, Cmnd 9524, London, HMSO.

Department of Education and Science (1987) *Higher Education: Meeting the Challenge*, Cm 114, London, HMSO.

Department of Education and Science (1988) *Statistical Bulletin 11/88*, London, Department of Education and Science.

Duke, C. (1986) 'Continuing education trends and policy implications', *Journal of Education Policy*, 1 (3), 255–70.

Evans, N. (1984) *Access to Higher Education: Non-standard Entry to CNAA First Degree and DipHE Courses*, CNAA Development Services Publication, London, Council for National Academic Awards.

Evans, N. (1985) *Post-Education Society: Recognizing Adults as Learners*, Beckenham, Croom Helm.

Fulton, O. (1981) 'Principles and policies' in O. Fulton (ed.) *Access to Higher Education*, Guildford, Society for Research into Higher Education.

Fulton, O. (1988) 'Elite survivals? Entry "standards" and procedures for higher education admissions', *Studies in Higher Education*, 13 (1), 15–25.

Further Education Unit (1987a) *Access to Further and Higher Education: A Discussion Document*, London, Further Education Unit.

Further Education Unit (1987b) *Black Students and Access to Higher Education: A Summary Document*, London, Further Education Unit.

Gibson, A. (1986) 'Providing for the learning needs of non-traditional students in higher education', *Journal of Access Studies*, 1 (2), 38–52.

Griffin, C. (1983) *Curriculum Theory in Adult and Lifelong Education*, Beckenham, Croom Helm.

Hutchinson, E. and Hutchinson, E. (1986) *Women Returning to Learning*, Cambridge, National Extension College.

Inner London Education Authority (1984) *Access to Higher Education: Report of Review of Access Courses at the Authority's Maintained Colleges of Further and Higher Education Carried Out in the Academic Year 1982/83 by Members of the Inspectorate*, London, Inner London Education Authority.

Jones, B. and Johnson, R. (1983) 'New horizons: an introduction to university studies', *Adult Education*, 56 (3), 218–26.

Jones, H. A. and Williams, K. E. (1979) *Adult Students and Higher Education*, Leicester, Advisory Council for Adult and Continuing Education.

Kearney, A. and Diamond, J. (1987) 'Access courses: a model for discussion', *Journal of Access Studies*, 2 (2), 33–43.

Lieven, M. (1987) 'Access courses and the adult residential colleges', *Journal of Access Studies*, 2 (1), 72–81.

Lieven, M. (1988) 'The liberal progressive movement and access to higher education', *Higher Education Review*, 20 (3), 61–9.

Lucas, S. and Ward, P. (eds) (1985) *A Survey of 'Access' Courses in England*, Lancaster, University of Lancaster School of Education.

Lyon, S. (1988) 'Unequal opportunities: Black minorities and access to higher education', *Journal of Further and Higher Education*, 12 (3), 21–37.

Michaels, R. (1986) 'Entry routes for mature students: variety and quality assessed', *Journal of Access Studies*, 1 (1), 57–71.

Millins, P. K. C. (1984) *Access Studies to Higher Education (September 1979–December 1983): A Report*, London, Roehampton Institute of Higher Education.

Millins, K., Reyersbach, S. and Yates, J. (1985) *Access Studies to Higher Education: Conference Report*, London, Roehampton Institute of Higher Education.

National Advisory Body (1988) *Action for Access: Widening Opportunities in Higher Education*, London, National Advisory Body for Public Sector Higher Education.

Neave, G. (1982a) 'On the edge of the abyss', *European Journal of Education*, 17 (2), 123–42.

Neave, G. (1982b) 'The changing boundary between the state and higher education', *European Journal of Education*, 17 (3), 231–41.

Neave, G. (1985) 'Elite and mass higher education in Britain: a regressive model?', *Comparative Education Review*, 29 (3), 347–61.

Osborne, M. (1988) 'Access courses in mathematics, science and technology: current and planned provision', *Journal of Access Studies*, 3 (1), 64–74.

Parry, G. (1986) 'From patronage to partnership', *Journal of Access Studies*, 1 (1), 43–53.

Parry, G. (1989) *Access and Preparatory Courses Offered By or In Association With the Universities*, London, Standing Conference on University Entrance.

Pelissier, C. and Smith, R. (1988) 'Student centred continuing education: a county strategy for access', *Journal of Further and Higher Education*, 12 (2), 64–71.

Percy, K. (1985) 'Adult learners in higher education' in C. Titmus (ed.) *Widening the Field: Continuing Education in Higher Education*, Guildford, SRHE and NFER-Nelson.

Percy, K. (1988) 'Opening access to a modern university' in H. Eggins (ed.) *Restructuring Higher Education*, Milton Keynes, Society for Research into Higher Education and Open University Press.

Percy, K. A., Powell, J. and Flude, C. (1983) *Students in the Open College of the North West: A Follow-up Study*, Blagdon, Coombe Lodge.

Royal Society of Arts (1988) *Raising the Standard: Wider Access to Higher Education*, London, Royal Society of Arts Industry Matters.

Schuller, T., Tight, M. and Weil, S. (1988) 'Continuing education and the redrawing of boundaries', *Higher Education Quarterly*, 42 (4), 335–52.

Slowey, M. (1988) 'Adult students – the new mission for higher education?', *Higher Education Quarterly*, 42 (4), 301–16.

Smithers, A. G. and Griffin, A. (1986) *The Progress of Mature Students*, Manchester, Joint Matriculation Board.

Squires, G. (ed.) (1983) *Innovation through Recession*, Guildford, Society for Research into Higher Education.

Tight, M. (1987) 'The value of higher education: full-time or part-time?', *Studies in Higher Education*, 12 (2), 169–85.

Tight, M. (1988) 'Access and part-time undergraduate study', *Journal of Access Studies*, 2 (1), 12–24.

Tight, M. (forthcoming) 'Access – not access courses', *Journal of Access Studies*.

Tolley, G. (1980) 'Access, community and curriculum' in N. Evans (ed.) *Education Beyond School: Higher Education for a Changing Context*, London, Grant McIntyre.

Toyne, P. (1979) *Education Credit Transfer: Feasibility Study*, London, Department of Education and Science.

Toyne, P. (1982) 'The Educational Counselling and Credit Transfer Information Service' in G. Squires (ed.) *Innovation through Recession*, Guildford, Society for Research into Higher Education.

Trow, M. (1974) 'Problems in the transition from elite to mass higher education' in OECD *Policies for Higher Education*, Paris, Organization for Economic Co-operation and Development.

Trow, M. (1981) 'Comparative perspectives on access' in O. Fulton (ed.) *Access to Higher Education*, Guildford, Society for Research into Higher Education.

Trow, M. (1987) 'Academic standards and mass higher education', *Higher Education Quarterly*, 41 (3), 268–91.

Trow, M. (1989) 'The Robbins Trap: British attitudes and the limits of expansion', *Higher Education Quarterly*, 43 (1), 55–75.

Unit for the Development of Adult Continuing Education (1988) *Developing Access: The Discussion Paper*, Leicester, Unit for the Development of Adult Continuing Education.

Usher, R. S. (1986) 'Reflection and prior work experience: some problematic issues in relation to adult students and university studies', *Studies in Higher Education*, 11 (3), 245–56.

Williams, J. and Bristow, S. with Housee, S. and Green, P. (1988) 'Access and success: mature students' perceptions of further education and higher education', *Journal of Access Studies*, 3 (1), 44–63.

Woodley, A. (1987) 'Has the Open University been an unqualified success?', *Journal of Access Studies*, 2 (2), 7–14.

Woodley, A., Wagner, L., Slowey, M., Hamilton, M. and Fulton, O. (1987) *Choosing to Learn: Adults in Education*, Milton Keynes, Society for Research into Higher Education and Open University Press.

Woodrow, M. (1988) 'The access course route to higher education', *Higher Education Quarterly*, 42 (4), 317–34.

3

Admissions, Access and Institutional Change

Oliver Fulton and Susan Ellwood

Introduction

This chapter, like others in this book, takes for granted the desirability of substantially widening access to higher education. Its concern is, rather, the feasibility of doing so. Fulton and others have argued elsewhere (Neave 1985; Fulton 1988; Trow 1989) that the British system does not – yet – deserve the label of mass higher education but is, in fact, in Neave's words, 'élite higher education written a little larger'. And nowhere is this clearer than in the procedures of selection for, or – in the customary and revealing phrase – admission to, higher education. In this chapter we draw on a recent study,[1] funded by the Training Agency, of admissions policy and practice in England and Wales. The study aimed to map the present pattern of admissions policies and practices, to examine the rationales, constraints and incentives affecting them, and so to assess the potential for an increase in the participation rate.

Admissions to higher education cannot be seen in isolation. As Trow first argued in 1974, access policies form one thread, if a crucial one, in a web of interlocking attitudes and values, and of the structures and policies which exemplify them – strands which in normal circumstances are mutually reinforcing. Much of our evidence shows that this was as true in 1988 as it ever was in the past. On the one hand there are now powerful pressures for change, with the call for wider access as their central theme: but on the other, the combination of entrenched values, established administrative procedures and rewards for success by the limited criteria of a long-standing élite system makes for a powerful set of resistances.

We begin by describing the main pressures and incentives for change, and then in the second section turn to the resistances and impediments. In each case we describe how these are experienced and interpreted by those directly involved in admissions. In the third section we discuss some of the changes, many of them quite modest, which we found in our study, and which might help to move us towards a larger, more comprehensive and more open system. The kinds of changes which we discuss in this chapter are quite varied. But underlying them all is the possibility of escape from the 'Robbins Trap' (Trow 1989), the central feature of which, from an access point of view, is the dominance of young people with A levels as the basic clientele of higher education.

Incentives to change

In the late 1980s a number of different influences, mainly external to higher education, began to emerge and to create, if not a consensus, at least a powerful constituency arguing in favour not only of a sharp expansion of access nationally, but of changes in specific admissions policies and practices. These influences include: patterns of demand and demography; pressures for social equality; changes in secondary education; patterns of employment; financing mechanisms; and the declining credibility of A levels.

Patterns of demand and demography

As is well known, the rate of demand for places for *full-time study* remained obstinately at or below fourteen per cent of the 18-year-old age group from the early 1970s to the mid-1980s,[2] but has recently begun to rise modestly. At the same time, however, that age group, from which a large majority of full-time students are still drawn, increased throughout the 1970s but began to fall gently in 1983 – although the major decline is still to come in the early 1990s. Thus the absolute demand for full-time places rose slowly throughout the period when the age participation rate (APR) was stagnant and it has not yet fallen, but will certainly do so in the next few years unless the participation rate – of 18-year-olds, of older people, or of both – increases considerably more than it has done so far. There are a number of reasons for expecting a modest increase (Department of Education and Science 1986); but present trends do not suggest a major shift towards mass participation in full-time courses.

Among our interviewees, admission officers' (AOs) and admission tutors' (ATs) experience and expectations of demand for full-time places varied substantially, depending on their institutions and subjects: but the majority had so far found little difficulty in recruitment. 'We've been anticipating a change that hasn't come', said a fairly typical polytechnic AO; while many university AOs described still rising demand from well-qualified A-level candidates. ATs in most higher-education institutions (HEIs) and most subjects (exceptions are discussed below) were, if anything, even more nonchalant. Their primary role is to handle the current year's admissions, not to think far ahead; if they had done so, the gentle start to the demographic downturn and the general buoyancy of demand had on the whole created a strong sense of security.

At the same time, the demand for *part-time* study has been rising in recent years. In the early 1970s, when the term 'academic drift' was coined by Burgess and Pratt, polytechnics were accused, among other sins, of shifting their interest in recruitment from part-time to full-time students. But although full-time numbers have increased in the polytechnics and colleges (PC) sector both before and after 1981 (when university full-time places were sharply cut back and polytechnics successfully accommodated most of those rejected), there has also been very substantial growth in part-time numbers in recent years. By no means all polytechnics and CHEs have been equally active in this market in the past: some made it a major emphasis well before the awareness of the demographic threat, but others are recent converts. In any event, AOs from nearly all the PC-sector institutions we visited now saw part-time students, whose age range tends to be older and wider than that of full-timers, as a major cushion against the possible consequences of demographic decline in the future.

But if the general view of future demand was, bluntly, complacent, this still conceals much variability. Even among the universities, where in 1988 the total number of full-time applications showed little or no sign of falling off, there were differences. Some university AOs were confident that any decline would never affect them: indeed two told us they could imagine considerable increases in numbers if there were no limits to places. And the 'leading' universities, which achieve very high average A-level scores (up to 13–15 points), recruiting large proportions of their students from independent or selective schools, feel confident that demographic decline will leave these schools untouched. At worst (in their terms) AOs from these universities anticipated making a modest drop in standard offers if necessary, but were not looking to make significant changes in recruitment practices or course structures, except perhaps in the most problematic subject areas.

Others, however, were experimenting – or preparing to experiment – with some changes both in course offerings and admissions policies, at least partly in response to demographic uncertainty: 'We think you should have plenty of buckets [of potential students] around.' Only one out of nine university AOs claimed to be entirely unconcerned by the demographic forecasts. (Moreover, Universities' Central Council on Admissions (UCCA) data show that even in 1987 there were few, if any, universities in which all subjects could sustain their standard offers across the board at results time.) But none of the universities, and very few departments within them, expected the 1990s to make a drastic difference. Any changes they anticipated were essentially quite marginal, or were primarily responses to other pressures than demography.

Many polytechnics – perhaps five out of the nine in our sample – and at least one large CHE were experiencing a similarly buoyant demand, although there were certainly departmental[3] exceptions, and most polytechnic AOs were also optimistic. For some, this was based on their success in competing with universities for 18-year-olds with A levels. But their take-up rates for this group are much lower, and optimism was more often based on experience of students from outside the 18-year-old A-level market – predominantly locally based, mature and part-time – and therefore out of the competition with universities. It was clear, moreover, from these more confident AOs that such a local or regional and part-time emphasis had generally developed well before awareness of the demographic threat. The other polytechnics and large colleges which felt they were facing more serious recruitment problems were moving sharply to diversify their provision: those with a strong local or part-time bias joining the national market, and vice versa. And the smaller CHEs were less buoyant: their volume of applications for full-time courses, on which they concentrate, was significantly lower, and the overall picture was stable at best. Contrasts between different subjects were particularly marked here. All of them were increasingly aware of the need to build up local links.

However, it was between subjects that the sharpest differences were to be found; and these could be seen in every institution. We interviewed ATs from eleven subject areas: architecture, biology, business studies, computing, education, electrical engineering, English, law, mathematics, sociology/social work and Spanish. Among these, the subjects with the highest levels of demand were business studies, English, law and sociology/social work. They each handled their applications quite differently: while law and business studies mainly gave preference to young A-level candidates, English and sociology/social work had a strong tradition, from well before demographic decline, of accepting mature and non-traditional applicants, not only out of a sense of social responsibility or in response to the substantial demand from such applicants, but also because they regarded them as excellent students in their own right. And unlike law and business studies, they were not prepared to be deflected from accepting older students by the increasing competition for places they were now experiencing from A-level candidates.

Among the subjects in our survey with greater recruitment problems, education, though suffering from considerable uncertainty about the level of demand, had a well-established tradition of receptiveness to 'nonstandard' applicants, but had recently been constrained by quotas imposed by the Council for the Accreditation of Teacher Education (CATE) and not of its own choosing. Spanish, on the other hand, had been able to respond positively to a sharp change in applications: the number of candidates with Spanish A levels has dropped substantially, not so much because of demographic change or a lack of demand, as because of the loss of school sixth forms capable of offering Spanish A levels. Most departments had simply abandoned their insistence on Spanish A levels and were now prepared to teach the subject *ab initio*, though mainly as part of a joint modern languages degree.

The other subjects we surveyed all contain a substantial mathematics or science component and have therefore suffered from the lower ratios of applicants to places which have been encouraged by a series of government-inspired 'switches' or 'steers' of higher-education places towards science and technology, combined with the limited supply of young people with mathematics and science A levels. However, these subjects' responses varied considerably. Biology was probably the least affected by a shortage of applicants; its public image is improving, it recruits reasonably well from women as well as men, and even, in some departments, from mature applicants. In general, application rates, while not always adequate, were improving. Computing had begun to adapt to shortages: in the PC sector at least, some departments did not insist on maths or physics A levels.

But mathematics and, perhaps more surprisingly, electrical engineering were disinclined, especially in universities, to change their traditional requirements – even at the price of empty places. Mathematics departments in universities were often very hostile to admitting mature candidates, and even in the PC sector mature students' numbers were very small; but some polytechnic and college departments had begun admitting candidates without maths A levels. Similarly, university electrical-engineering departments were reluctant to consider even applicants with BTEC qualifications, regarding them as underqualified in the theoretical aspects of physics and engineering, and unwilling to adapt their courses to cope with these deficiencies. Both they and also the polytechnic and college departments recruited quite small numbers of mature students, mainly under 25 years old. However, some polytechnic and college departments were prepared to accept both the new Technology A levels and relevant AS levels. (One regarded AS levels as 'manna from heaven': 'It gives us a reasonable excuse for lowering our entry qualifications.') In general, however, the number of departments in these two subjects prepared to alter their entry requirements, to the extent of adapting their courses for new kinds of entrants, was quite small.

To summarize, we found two rather contradictory trends. On the one hand, there is considerable confidence in the system as a whole: there were few AOs who were seriously worried about their institutions' viability either at present or indeed in the 1990s, and they generally felt that further developments in part-time and continuing education (to which they were often strongly committed for their own sake) would cope with any short-falls in their institutions as a whole. On the other hand, there was probably no institution in which AOs were satisfied about the viability of every department, even in 1988; and coupled with the other causes for uncertainty, to which we now turn, there was in many an underlying uneasiness about the future, if not yet a positive commitment to major change.

Pressures for social equality

In policy discussions the earlier emphasis on the responsibility of education for promoting social equality has been distinctly muted in recent years. Within government, its chief promoter was, until its abolition, the Manpower Services/Training Commission, which developed a strong equal opportunities policy partly in response to the interests of the Commission's membership but also out of a concern for the greatest possible development and use of scarce talent. However, the 1985 Green Paper (Department of Education and Science 1985) was pointedly low-key on the subject, and the 1987 White Paper (Department of Education and Science 1987), though much more enthusiastic about access, was quite explicitly inspired by labour-market needs and not by considerations of social justice or the rights of citizenship. However, during 1988 and 1989 Department of Education and Science (DES) ministers have begun to make amends, by making strongly positive statements about the need to promote access for underrepresented groups including women, ethnic minorities and working-class people.

In our survey, we asked about attitudes to such groups. We wanted to know both what ATs' and AOs' attitudes were when they received applications from people from these backgrounds, and also whether they were satisfied with the kinds of applicants they were getting. Most of our interviewees, products of the 1960s and 1970s, were certainly sympathetic in principle to the claims of social justice, and nearly all AOs and many ATs told us they wanted, in the words of one, to 'make space' for non-traditional or less well-qualified applicants – though many of them found it difficult to do so for reasons we shall turn to later. Most of these were well aware of, and claimed to be dissatisfied with, the broad profile of their student intake. They generally expressed a rather vague desire for 'more' of various underrepresented groups, but, in the same breath, questioned their ability to influence the kinds of students who applied to them. At best they and their colleagues were increasing their involvement in 'outreach' such as schools liaison work. But much of this is of a very general nature. It may appease an institution's or department's conscience, but it generally does not result in any new mechanisms to change the balance of applicants or entrants.

However, we did find some institutions and departments with admissions policies designed to deliver wider recruitment – mainly PC-sector institutions drawing on a local as well as a national market for students, and humanities or social-science departments responding to well-established non-traditional demand. The PC institutions had often been strongly encouraged by their local education authorities' equal-opportunities policies. Some examples are given in the final section.

Changes in secondary education

The last few years have seen a large number of changes in secondary education, many of which have implications for entrants to higher

education in the near future, even if their impact has not yet been felt.[4] The
most obvious of these are the changes in teaching and assessment pre-16,
which were pioneered by the introduction and gradual spread of TVEI,
and are now formalized in the shift from O levels/CSE to GCSE with its
much greater emphasis on student-centred learning, project and investigative work and so on. Current plans for universal records of achievement
could in the medium term have even more radical effects, if they were to
lead to the eventual abolition of examinations at 16, as some of their
proponents hope.

Although A levels have been formally preserved for the time being from
the reforms proposed by the Higginson Committee (see below), thoughtful
AOs and ATs whom we interviewed were conscious that changes in pre-16
education are bound to have a knock-on effect on A levels: in the kind of
teaching that GCSE holders will expect – not only in the sixth form or its
equivalent but in higher education as well; in the balance of skills that they
possess; and probably in gaps in their knowledge of a formal curriculum
that was previously taken for granted. In other words, within a few years
young entrants to higher education may well be far better learners, but the
kinds of basic knowledge and abstract operational skills which are now
taken for granted are likely to be more patchy. How serious a problem this
will pose is unclear. We were struck by the almost universal approval which
those who had come across it gave to the International Baccalaureate (IB)
as an entry qualification. The IB has, in fact, many of the qualities just
described but was generally regarded as excellent preparation for almost
any course for which it was offered. Possibly the kinds of schools which
teach the IB provide some reassurance.

Ironically, in 1988 most ATs were largely unaware of these developments. Admittedly, TVEI pilot schemes only affected a minority of schools
or colleges and a minority of pupils within them, and in any case TVEI does
not incorporate separate named qualifications; and GCSE is so recent that
they would not have seen it on application forms in 1988. And even AS
levels, which will have a much more direct impact, were so new that,
although departments might have made formal policy statements, few ATs
had yet had opportunity to put them into effect. Still, we were surprised by
the level of ignorance among most of our interviewees: although the days
of A levels are not yet numbered, it is clear that change is in the air. It may
not be many years before not only admissions procedures but course
structures and content face major changes: we saw few signs that most
institutions were preparing for them.

Patterns of employment

Whatever its economic underpinnings, the growth in demand for graduates from the labour market in the second half of the 1980s has had
profound political consequences. After the relative stagnation of the 1970s,

in which there were significant levels of unemployment in various disciplines, and demand in general barely kept up with the increasing supply, the recession of the early 1980s merely confirmed public and political hostility to higher education. The 1985 Green Paper, with its grudging acceptance ('the benefits must justify the cost') of the National Advisory Body (NAB) definition of access which emphasized 'ability to benefit' rather than formal qualifications, was the culmination of these doubts about the value to the economy of investment in graduate output. The years since then, with the highly visible shortages of graduates in some subjects, the huge growth in sectors such as financial services and the creation of the Council for Industry and Higher Education and other pressure groups, have been marked by a sharp turn-round in government attitudes. This was exemplified in the 1987 White Paper which accepted the need to expand access, not only by raising the APR of young people but also by opening up opportunities for older entrants, mainly through Access courses; and even more dramatically in the Secretary of State's Lancaster speech of January 1989 which talked of an APR of thirty per cent as an achievable medium-term goal. There are certainly unresolved questions about the depth of government's or employers' commitment to expansion – in particular how and by whom it is to be financed. But, even if it turns out to be short-lived, the national policy climate in 1988 was very different from that of five years earlier.

From the standpoint of hard-pressed admissions tutors, these changes may well have seemed both remote and superficial; and our questions did not, to be fair, address national policy directly. But we could not avoid the impression that most ATs' approaches to their departments' policy and practice were more dominated by the restrictive past than by the more expansionist future that might have been in prospect. It is perfectly true that, whatever the content of national policy discussions, the signals from the national funding bodies were at best mixed and at worst downright discouraging, as we show later. But we were surprised and a little disheartened to find so much emphasis on where students were coming from to fill existing places on existing terms, and so little, even from AOs, on the possibilities for radical expansion.

Financing mechanisms

As we shall argue shortly, present financing mechanisms are more of an impediment than an incentive to expanding access to higher education: in 1988, institutions – and departments – might be penalized, and would certainly gain nothing but extra demands on their resources, if they exceeded fixed quotas of places. This was true, at least, for home students on degree and other qualification-bearing courses. But it was conspicuously not true for other kinds of students – notably those from overseas and those on any short courses which were not planned and financed by the funding bodies. For each of these, institutions have for some time been free, indeed expected, to charge 'full cost', or perhaps more accurately, market rates of fees. Our main concern was home students on qualification-bearing courses, and we did not normally ask about these other categories; but a number of AOs and ATs mentioned them to us, primarily to illustrate the very different policies which applied in these cases.

Some institutions were already using short courses, often commissioned or block-booked by particular employers, as a substantial revenue-raising activity; and a few designed them so that individual students could also be given academic credit for their work, using modular credit-accumulation schemes which could eventually lead to qualifications. In this way, these institutions, which included universities as well as polytechnics, were able to enhance access for individuals as well as increasing their own revenue.

Overseas students are a sensitive topic, since there is a potential conflict between the normal (home) admissions criterion of the highest attainable pre-entry qualification, and the alternative of ability to pay the fees demanded. Some ATs were uncomfortable with the pressure they felt from their central administrations to admit overseas students with qualifications which they would have rejected from home applicants: such pressure, one told us, often 'gets in the way of right judgment'. Nevertheless, it is clear that under these circumstances extra places are being found, and less well-qualified students are being taught – one hopes with reasonable success.

There can be little doubt that a variety of systems of funding could be devised which encouraged institutions to maximize their intake: indeed press reports in March 1989 indicated that the PCFC was considering various alternative schemes which might do so. The consequences are difficult to predict: much will depend, no doubt, on the finance available to students – another undecided policy issue at the time of writing. It is conceivable that the net effect would not be to increase total numbers but simply to shift a fixed pool of students from one institution to another – with unpredictable effects on the quality of teaching and learning. But it seems likely that there will be some relaxation in the financial disincentives to extra recruitment under which institutions have generally operated up to now. Such a relaxation may well be a necessary, if not sufficient, condition for the expansion of access.

Although, as we show later, lack of resources was blamed by many AOs and ATs for their inability to do all they would like to improve access, the examples above demonstrate that financial need can also push even reluctant institutions or departments into new initiatives. In particular, as we shall see, some kinds of modular course restructuring, though originally prompted by the need to cut costs, are already proving important for widening access.

The declining credibility of A levels

In the last few years, criticisms of A levels have intensified. Indeed, the

Higginson Committee's Report of 1988 embodied a virtual consensus in favour of substantial reform which would have seemed astonishing only a few years earlier – a consensus, however, that was not powerful enough to overrule other pressures on the government of the day. Criticisms have focused on four main problem areas for those taking A levels (Fulton 1988): overspecialization, pedagogic style, potential bias (from unequal access to teaching resources) and reliability of grading. A further concern is the worry that, partly for structural reasons, partly because they are unattractive to 16-year-olds, the continued existence of A levels may unduly restrict the pool of potential entrants to higher education.

The first two problem areas have obvious implications for the content and method of courses in higher education, while the second two challenge the fairness of the selection process. As Mortimore and Mortimore (1989) point out, vice-chancellors – unlike their predecessors faced with earlier reform proposals – were among the leaders in deploring the government's rejection of the proposed reforms. Their concerns were mainly over-specialization and learning styles, though the anxiety about restricting demand also played a part.

We suggested above that changes in secondary schools, if carried through, may eventually have an unavoidable impact on the content and style of A levels – but that AOs and ATs on the whole were unaware of them. However, many of those we interviewed were concerned with the fairness problem, acknowledging that there are indeed sharp school, social-class and regional differences in A-level achievements, and that they are often poor predictors of subsequent performance. And yet, as we describe in the next section, many of them then slipped unconsciously into the language of 'standards', of which they saw A levels as one of the main guarantees. This contradictory set of views suggests that, contrary to the hopes of many reformers, A levels – and all that they imply in terms not only of educational content but also of the limited clientele of higher education – are far from doomed. In the next section we turn to some of the reasons why this is the case.

Impediments to change

One of our key findings, and probably the most troubling for advocates of expanding access, was that virtually throughout the system, and even among the minority of our interviewees (both AOs and ATs) facing serious recruitment difficulties, the commonest response has been to try to increase their 'market share' from a fixed and diminishing pool of 'good' A-level candidates rather than to try to widen the pool by increasing the total amount of demand. From the point of view of the system as a whole, these efforts are totally wasted, since they imply competition in, at best, a zero-sum game. Indeed, despite all the uncertainties about social-class-specific participation rates, rising participation by women and so on, they are disturbingly likely to lead to a drop in the total number of students in the near future. It is tempting to blame this behaviour on inertia or, worse still, on ignorance. But our interviews clearly show that, given the present rules of the game, it is by no means irrational.

Academic values and assumptions

We commented above that our interviewees' views of A levels were often a less than consistent combination of anxieties about their meaning and reliability with a reiteration of the importance of high 'standards'. It would be possible to interpret this as an example of the imperviousness of entrenched values to factual evidence; indeed many critics would see such attitudes as encapsulating the not only élite but élitist nature of British higher education. We found ATs congratulating themselves on rising A-level points as indicating not so much rising demand – which is undeniable – as rising quality – despite their low correlation with degree results, of which these same people were often well aware. Remarks such as 'We accept the best students we can', or 'Our policy is to recruit high-quality students' were commonplace, using A levels as the measure. One AO even told us explicitly, and others clearly assumed, that A-level students are 'cleverer' than access-course students. But the number of people with systematic information from their own courses to back up these claims was very small. As we show later, very few monitored the progress of students with different qualifications, and those that did so generally found good justification for widening, not restricting, their intake. Thus, although Peter Wright (Chapter 7 of this volume) can assert with justice that 'it would be quite implausible to explain the continued predominance of . . . [A levels] . . . as resulting from evidence that they represent . . . the skills and knowledge needed for the successful completion of a degree course', a large majority of our interviewees would not only claim exactly that, but would add that the higher the grade, the better the preparation.

External support for élitist values

There is, of course, no such thing as a pure value system, held independently of social conditions. And the attitudes to 'standards' which we have described have powerful structural supports. In the university sector the most important of these is the use of admissions statistics for resource allocation, both inside and outside the institution. Whatever the public statements of the University Grants Committee (UGC) and Committee of Vice-Chancellors and Principals (CVCP), whose working parties have pointedly dropped entry grades from their list of proposed performance indicators (PIs), most AOs were convinced that standard offers and average A-level-points scores of entrants are still used as a key indicator of both departmental and institutional quality, and produced chapter and verse to prove it to their own satisfaction. Perhaps especially in the light of talk about 'superleagues' of universities, with their implications, under possible new funding arrangements, for teaching as well as research, neither AOs nor ATs see it as in their interests to allow standard offers or entrants' points scores to sink below the highest achievable level. Admittedly, PC sector AOs and ATs were less conscious of the same pressure: but by no means all were immune from it, still less from the less consciously held values which go with it.

To say this is not to transfer all the responsibility to the funding councils. Apart from the fact that most of the latter's members and advisers are themselves academics, who presumably bring their own values to bear on their choice of PIs, all of the internal processes of student assessment in higher education depend on placing a high value on norm-referenced measures of achievement; it is extremely difficult for teachers, however sophisticated, to ignore previous test results. Moreover, lay people – the public, politicians and directly interested parties such as employers and professional associations – are implicated in the same value system. There is research evidence (Roizen and Jepson 1985) to show that in the early 1980s employers used A-level entry points – input measures – as the key indicator of the standards of an institution's output. Some of the professional associations, too, still set minimum standards for entry as a condition of accrediting a department's courses. In each case the implications are distinctly insulting to higher education and its students, and leave no space for the concept of the 'value added' to individual students by their experience of degree courses. Nevertheless, the attitudes persist; perhaps the best hope is that the gathering shortage of graduates, and the impending shortage of 'good' A-level candidates will lead both academics and employers to recognize talent wherever they find it.

Financing policies

Academic considerations aside, there is another strong reason for maintaining a high A-level emphasis – also the result of policies of the funding bodies.[5] In the university sector there has been a consistent UGC policy, enforced most notoriously in 1981, of 'preserving the unit of resource' by restricting intake numbers to fixed quotas, and either penalizing departments or institutions that exceed them or, at a minimum, ensuring that no extra resources will be made available. As a result, as one university AO put it, 'For a course with 50 places, the last thing you want in our present funding arrangements, is more than 50 flaming students . . . 51 and I'm doing that one for free.'

In the PC sector the same broad policy has applied since the advanced further education (AFE) funding 'pool' was 'capped' and the NAB took over resource allocation – though with the difference that as numbers were rising many institutions and courses chose to exceed their quotas modestly to make a case for an increased quota the next year (see Wagner, Chapter 9). Even so, most polytechnics and colleges have also carefully monitored their numbers, for internal purposes at least. One polytechnic AO told us that 'the only [admissions] policy is to admit the right number of students to courses: that in itself is a sufficiently massive task.' Unfortunately, if numbers are to be controlled, A levels are particularly well suited to the job: offers can be marginally adjusted from year to year to yield the required numbers, whereas qualifications such as Access courses (so long as they are unranked – see Brennan, Chapter 4) do not 'map on to' A-level grades and cannot be up- or downgraded to adjust to changing demand.

'Consumer' accountability

A further practical reason why so many ATs retain their emphasis on A levels despite the counter-pressures and, in some cases, their better judgement, is that A levels are a standard, well-known, 'legitimated' currency. More than half of the AOs we interviewed and many ATs expressed anxiety about any suggestion of positive discrimination (though we did not use the word) – that is of rejecting those with the highest grades, or even varying offers in the light of individual backgrounds, explaining that schools and 'increasingly consumerist' applicants and their parents would certainly protest, and they would have no clear defence on individual cases. Lawsuits such as the Bakke case in the United States were clearly in their mind; and ATs from many university departments, heavily reliant on independent schools and anxious to preserve good relations with them, were for this reason unwilling to consider compensating for their students' undoubted advantages. Certainly, the increased competition of the last few years has focused more attention on the level of offers. Potential candidates feel, understandably, that they have a right to know how they will be judged, and the universities have recently responded to the growth industry in unofficial guides by publishing an 'official guide' to entrance offers against which applicants can compare themselves.

Organizational and administrative issues

It is a curious irony that, so far as we can tell, admissions is, in most institutions, one of the less important areas of institutional policy. Partly this is a consequence of the restricted supply of places referred to above: in recent years there have been few, if any, major institutions whose future might have been threatened by a shortage of students, and the pressure to keep up A-level scores which we have described leads more to constant vigilance than to major policy initiatives. But it is also a sign of the paradox which one of us has discussed elsewhere (Fulton 1988), that an apparently élite system, which pays homage to the idea of individual selection with all the paraphernalia of character references and personal decision-making by academic staff, should yet have formalized and routinized most of its admissions procedures. (Interviewing, for example, has declined sharply in recent years.[6])

There are plenty of examples of the rather low standing of admissions policy and practice. To start with the most ceremonial, by no means all the institutions we visited, and only two universities, could quote us a formal admissions-policy statement. Some AOs, particularly but not only in the universities, offered us rather bland personal statements and, when pressed, denied any central policy involvement – 'the departments make the policy'. (Moreover, any policy themes they did identify had more to do with numbers and 'quality' than access.) Six polytechnics, however, and two large and one small CHE had established (and others were preparing) formal statements, which generally declared wider access as the key element, the characteristic themes being 'ability to benefit' and 'equal opportunity'.

But whatever the formal statements, throughout our sample it was quite unusual for institutional policy to override departments' own internal policy and procedures. Within most institutions we found wide variations in departments' policies, with regard to all aspects of access and recruitment as well as admissions procedures. For most AOs, this was a matter not so much of constitutional autonomy as of common sense: 'The courses are essentially different, some courses are more appealing to people in certain groups, other courses are less appealing.' At their sternest, AOs tolerated variation '. . . provided that they bear in mind the overall policies on ethnic, women and special needs.' The AOs from institutions with strong policy statements recognized this as a sensitive area: 'We can't force [departments]. If they . . . fill up the course with A levels year in year out and meet their target, well fine . . . [but] . . . what I want to do is persuade them . . . that when [Access] students come forward . . . they should be given a fair crack of the whip and that if they aren't then we'll probably establish quotas.'

Except for overseas students, every institution in our sample was either opposed, or at best reluctant, to impose quotas, even for 'non-standard' entrants. One polytechnic had tried to promote the idea of self-imposed rather than centrally mandated quotas, but even this had been sharply resisted; but a few others had taken the plunge and allocated firm quotas to at least some of their courses. But these were exceptions; in most places institutional policy is in reality the sum of the policies of separate departments. It is not surprising that departments, in their turn, often felt quite uncertain about institutional policy, with some ATs complaining of a lack of clear direction and of 'scattered initiatives', and others of conflicting messages.

In addition, we found that the concept of 'policy' in relation to admissions was as foreign in departments as it was in many institutions. Unless there was a crisis of recruitment or reorganization, departments rarely discussed admissions, but left it to the AT, possibly in occasional liaison with the head of department or central AO. Most ATs simply did not think of their work in policy terms: rather, their main task was a complex administrative one. Their colleagues, they told us, expected them to fill, but not overshoot, the target allocation; to keep the average-points score high; and to admit those students who they believed could cope most easily with the existing course with the least possible alteration to content or to teaching methods. It was only after all these requirements had been satisfied that they could turn their minds to enhancing access. It is not surprising, therefore, that the job of AT was treated by most departments not as a key decision-making post, but as one of a number of administrative chores, sometimes left with the same person for years, sometimes rotated frequently – but with little systematic training in either case.

Finally, if policy is to be implemented effectively, its outcomes must presumably be monitored – and this is another area of weakness. Certainly, all institutions collect some data on total applications and admissions numbers – the latter being essential for resource allocation. They also monitor entry qualifications, for the reasons outlined above, or for validation or course-review purposes. But many stop there; only a few in our sample conducted systematic and regular monitoring of their applications and admissions profiles in terms of gender, age, ethnicity, social class of parents, region of home or type of school. We found some places where such data was collected and was being used to 'persuade' departments as to the benefits of recruiting a wider social mix – though in the absence of stronger mechanisms the main method of persuasion seemed to be 'publicity and shame'.

Only a few institutions – three universities, one polytechnic, three large CHEs and one small CHE – followed up their monitoring by feeding the results back into the policy-making process. However, some polytechnics and larger CHEs were now planning to introduce comprehensive performance indicators (PIs) for admissions in their preparations for corporate status. About half of them – and two universities – even intended to collect longitudinal data in order to compare degree outcomes with entry qualifications. Moreover, at least one polytechnic was prepared to allocate some resources on the basis of the proportion of non-standard students admitted, while another hoped to introduce admissions outcomes in the validation process; but in the others it was not clear how they would deal with any shortcomings identified in reviews or monitoring.

At course or departmental level, some monitoring is well established in all CNAA-validated institutions as part of the review process and normally includes some form of cohort analysis of entry qualifications, student profiles and student progress. Although this should give review panels the opportunity to promote particular access policies, we found that often the admissions were taken as fixed, and data on student progress and outcomes were used to focus discussion on course content and teaching methods. However, in the small number of cases where ATs took such data seriously, they were able to use it very effectively to justify changes in their own admissions policy – almost always in the direction of widening access.

Resources for access

Probably all the institutions we visited see themselves as short of resources, with an increasing number of competing demands. Most access developments involve significant costs. Many AOs were worried by the resource implications of Access courses: '[In-house Access courses] . . . as an economic proposition [aren't] worth it, but as a political statement . . . and an educational statement [they] may well be worthwhile'; and four out of the nine polytechnic AOs could not foresee further in-house developments without extra earmarked funding; even supporting FE-based courses involved costs. The same applied to other kinds of course developments to meet the needs of new types of student. The problem is especially acute in the smaller CHEs, because of their small resource base, and in the universities, which find it difficult to justify investment in course development when faced with urgent demands to improve research quality. However, as we hinted earlier, some resource constraints have led to positive outcomes – and it is to positive examples, whatever their origins, that we now turn.

Good practice

In the previous section we have sketched a fairly formidable list of reasons why adapting for greater access has proved, and is still proving, so difficult for most institutions. The reader might be forgiven for thinking that little or nothing has occurred, or will, to shift us nearer to a mass-access system, with participation rates comparable with those of the leading industrialized countries. We end, therefore, with a number of promising developments which we found in different institutions – mainly but by no means exclusively in the polytechnics and colleges. A word of caution is appropriate, however. All the places we visited could give us lists, if of varying lengths, of course developments, one of the main areas of change. However, ascribing these, or any other changes, to self-conscious policies for access is more problematic: many were driven more by changing labour-market needs, by the availability of earmarked funding, or by efficiency considerations. And many of the changes may equally well have been aimed at improving an institution's attractiveness to, or its capacity to accommodate, the traditional student.

Access courses

Access courses are the subject of Chapter 4 of this book and will not be discussed in detail here. But it was clear to us that – in line with the White Paper's policy – they are the main instrument of active recruitment or admissions policies at the institutional level. Two-thirds of the universities, all the polytechnics and all but one of the CHEs in our sample had links with local Access courses run at further-education (FE) colleges, and about half (half the universities, most of the polytechnics and large CHEs, none of the small CHEs) also ran in-house Access courses. Both in-house and FE-based courses increasingly targeted particular groups, and some were backed by external funding (e.g. the European Social Fund). Although in the past many Access courses had been 'tied' by place guarantees to a particular course or institution, the general trend in our sample was to abandon place guarantees – partly because numbers were growing so fast that the guarantees could not be sustained much longer.

However, recent developments have gone beyond single courses. Several institutions (two universities, five polytechnics and two large CHEs) had become the focus for new regional access networks, mainly accreditation systems for Access courses of different kinds, taught in a number of FE colleges. In four polytechnics there were moves to 'franchise' degree-level work, mainly first-year courses, to a group of FE colleges, to make them available in more locations, and some AOs saw franchises as the first stage towards a regional 'credit consortium'. Finally, three universities, four polytechnics and three large CHEs were also involved either in the CNAA Credit Accumulation and Transfer Scheme (CATS) or in their own CAT scheme.

Paradoxically, the growth of Access courses is also the cause of some concern about a possible restriction of opportunities. A minority of institutions in our sample (four universities, the three small (university-validated) CHEs, one polytechnic and one large CHE) still had 'special entry' procedures for direct admissions to courses for people who do not meet 'general entry requirements'. As Access courses have proliferated, direct entry – which used to be common – is used less and less in the PC sector: indeed there is some suspicion that Access courses may now be recommended or required unnecessarily, as a convenient alternative, for the AT, to an individual assessment on limited evidence. Direct entry has been an important access route in the past and, if encouraged, could become increasingly so in the future as continuing-education initiatives and recognition of prior learning develop. It would be a pity if it were to be abandoned at this stage.

Modular course structures

Undoubtedly the most important forms of course restructuring to have taken place in the late 1980s are the moves towards modular-course structures which have occurred at a wide range of institutions. At their best, these offer students courses which can be virtually tailor-made to fit not only their interests but also their backgrounds and needs for preparation in different parts of a syllabus. The more flexible modular structures usually also permit varying modes of attendance and several award levels (e.g. diploma or certificate as well as degree). It is mainly polytechnics and, more recently, the larger CHEs which have pioneered modular structures, generally at first in a limited range of subjects – sometimes within departments, sometimes in broader groupings such as 'Combined Studies': but by summer 1988 four out of nine polytechnics in our sample and two of the four large CHEs had decided to move towards an institution-wide modular structure, and only one was actively resisting the idea.

Access has often been the key motive, though economy of teaching provision can be an added bonus. Although in general the universities were much less sympathetic, there were exceptions – and these were by no means the most vulnerable in their recruitment of traditional students. We found examples of collaboration within and outside the institution in credit accumulation and transfer; of new part-time variants of full-time degrees; and of modular first-year courses to permit remedial work, especially in mathematics and science; indeed, one university had recently decided to adopt an institution-wide modular course structure.

Departments varied in their receptiveness to, or enthusiasm for, modular reorganization. It is the humanities and social sciences which have been most active so far, areas which already have the most experience of admitting non-traditional students – but which have also needed to rationalize their course provision, or to provide more flexible links with vocational subjects in recent years. In science, engineering and technology departments progress was slower, though Credit Accumulation and Transfer Schemes (CATS) are growing in popularity. Here departments are worried about the reactions of employers and, especially, the professional associations. Modularity, by making space for remedial modules and encouraging breadth, can be accused both of reducing intake 'quality' and threatening coverage of key areas of the curriculum. But some ATs told us that employers were very supportive, welcoming both the opportunity to negotiate tailor-made short modules for their staff, and the new degree combinations of science or engineering with management and business.

Part-time study has long been designed to meet the needs of local, mainly mature students. In the past, it has mostly been offered as part-time degree courses completely separate from any full-time equivalents. Modularity is changing this; with some ingenuity, departments with modular structures can, and many do, offer a variety of modes of attendance, and avoid wasteful duplication of teaching. However, a more innovative use of modular structures is the kind of Associate Student Scheme which we found in five polytechnics and two universities in our sample. Here people without recent educational experience or formal qualifications can sample a course unit; assessment is optional but, if they choose to be assessed and are successful, they can enrol in the degree programme proper, often with credit exemption for their successfully completed module(s). However, as with Access courses, demand for some of these schemes had become so high that staff on popular courses were questioning the automatic right of entry. We can understand the practical difficulty, but the values or priorities implied are revealing. There can be no better test of suitability for degree-level work than success in passing a degree-level module.

In addition to full modular structures, diplomas and other qualifications below full degree level have an important part to play in improving access. For example, the DipHE was designed in part to provide access to PC-sector higher education for those without normal entry requirements. We found that one large CHE had recently remodelled its degree provision so that any student, including those who do not meet its General Entry Requirement (GER), can formally register at the outset for a DipHE, which may or may not lead on to a degree. Several polytechnics, too, were particularly keen to retain the DipHE, fearing that without it all under-qualified students would be referred to Access courses. In certain PC-sector departments the HND was a similar safety net for doubtful candidates: in one polytechnic fifty per cent of the HND students went on to enter a degree course. The CNAA is now encouraging all the institutions it validates to consider building in this sort of transferability, which is normally two-way, so that degree-course ATs can take greater risks with applicants, knowing that students in difficulties can transfer to the HND rather than failing outright. Moreover, the diplomas need not be provided in the same institution. We found two new instances of university–CHE collaboration, with a CHE providing DipHEs or HNDs tied directly to a specific degree course in a university. One AO described this as a unique opportunity to combine access with quality, commenting that seventy-five per cent of the CHE entrants finished at the HND level.

Organizational issues

In general, as we showed earlier, admissions policy is not a major policy-development area in institutions. In some, any commitments to wider access had been generated by committees primarily concerned with other areas such as equal opportunities or even publicity and public relations. However the formal admissions-policy statements we referred to earlier had generally been developed by, or had led to the formation of, 'access centres', central units involved in the formulation, development and, to varying degrees, implementation of policy. Four polytechnics and two universities in our sample had such units, with various titles. All but one tried to work through the institution's faculties, schools or departments, one seeing itself as 'the initiator, stimulator, facilitator . . . with the five Faculties in developing Access provision . . . [but] only working through

the Faculties', another as having a 'co-ordinating, information disseminating, intelligence gathering and disseminating kind of policy-setting role
rather than delivering activity per se'. Three access centres were also
responsible for providing staff development for admissions tutors and
others. (Few institutions without centres offered any staff development in
admissions.)

Course initiatives and outreach activities

Despite the generally gloomy picture of 'outreach' which we sketched
earlier, some institutions and departments were actively trying to widen
access by attracting new groups to apply to them. One polytechnic and one
large CHE, for example, were developing courses aimed at specific ethnic
groups in their local community (Irish studies, Caribbean studies, etc.).
Two polytechnics were developing information and guidance services,
notably one with a new and successful 'higher education shop' in the town
centre. A large CHE with a policy of outreach to community groups had
established a multi-cultural unit; had a women's working party; and
planned to establish a centre for the physically disabled within the college.
One of the small CHEs, however, mentioned its local ethnic minority
communities, but 'We're constrained by finance . . . and we haven't got
unlimited time to do the preparation.'

Conclusion

Despite the impression given by the last section of considerable activity,
especially in the PC sector, it must be added that on the whole the more
popular institutions and departments which competed successfully for
A-level candidates were less likely to adopt either access or outreach
initiatives. Although Chris Duke, in Chapter 10 of this book, describes a
university which, though highly successful both in recruitment and in
research, still takes access very seriously, it seems likely that further
incentives will be needed to encourage many of those in the strongest
position in the traditional A-level market to take major steps to broaden
their intake. Failing these, we are likely to see a system with much sharper
diversity and stratification between 'accessible' and 'traditional' institutions.
How well the former might serve the needs of the students who end up at
these very different institutions, let alone the cause of improving access to
the system as a whole, is a matter for speculation and debate. But given the
disincentives for change which we have identified, there must be serious
doubt whether participation will be increased to anything like the level
which is now agreed to be necessary.

Notes

1 During summer 1988 the authors and other fieldworkers interviewed admissions officers (AOs) or other senior management in twenty-five higher-education institutions (HEIs): nine universities, nine polytechnics, four large and three small colleges of higher education (CHEs); and over two hundred departmental admissions tutors (ATs) in eleven subject areas in the same institutions. Applications and admissions data from PCAS and UCCA for 1987 entry were also analysed. The project's main findings and recommendations are summarized in Fulton and Ellwood (1989), on which this chapter draws. The opinions expressed here are those of the authors, not the Training Agency.
2 Technically it is the age participation rate (APR) which is measured here. However, there is little evidence of substantial unsatisfied demand during the period.
3 Throughout the paper we use the term 'department' for convenience to refer also to all other teaching and organizational groupings such as course teams.
4 A useful summary of recent and prospective changes and their likely impact is given in Mortimore and Mortimore 1989.
5 Another aspect of funding-body policy which has long been a source of problems for access is the relative weighting given to full-time and various types of part-time students in resource-allocation formulas. Four polytechnic AOs made the point to us: 'If that [full-time] provision is where the loot is, [departments] are not going to be interested in . . . mature students if they don't get any money for them.'
6 There are noteworthy exceptions, including collegiate universities, subjects which wish to test non-written skills (languages, creative arts, social work, etc.) and certain other subjects – notably English in our sample – with conceptions of suitability for a course which go beyond the formal measurement of examination results. Many universities also interview all mature or non-traditional applicants, often for good reasons: but perhaps conveying to such candidates in the process a sense that they are intrinsically problematic.

References

Department of Education and Science (1985) *The Development of Higher Education into the 1990s*, Cmnd 9524, London, HMSO.
Department of Education and Science (1986) *Projections of Demand for Higher Education in Great Britain 1986–2000*, London, Department of Education and Science.
Department of Education and Science (1987) *Higher Education: Meeting the Challenge*, Cm. 114, London, HMSO.
Fulton, O. (1988) 'Elite survivals? Entry "standards" and procedures for higher education admissions', *Studies in Higher Education*, 13 (1).
Fulton, O. and Ellwood, S. (1989) *Admissions to Higher Education: Policy and Practice*, Sheffield, Department of Employment: The Training Agency.
Mortimore, P. and Mortimore, J. (1989) 'Changes in schooling: the impact on higher education', *Higher Education Quarterly*, 43 (1).
Neave, G. (1985) 'Elite and mass higher education in Britain: a regressive model?' *Comparative Education Review*, 29.

Roizen, J. and Jepson, M. (1985) *Degrees for Jobs: Employer Expectations of Higher Education*, Guildford, SRHE and NFER–Nelson.
Trow, M. (1989) 'The Robbins Trap: British attitudes and the limits of expansion', *Higher Education Quarterly*, 43 (1).

4

Access Courses

John Brennan

The object of intense debate in some parts of UK higher education while virtually ignored in others, Access courses are gaining increasing recognition among politicians and other system managers as providing an answer to perceived problems of 'participation' in higher education in the 1990s. However, as we shall see, this official 'stamp of approval' to what has been a rapidly expanding movement within further and higher education over the last decade is far from being an unambiguous endorsement of its values and objectives. The response within higher education to those values and objectives is itself uncertain, particularly given the changing agendas within institutions as new systems of governance and funding are set in place.

In this chapter we shall look at the Access-course 'movement' both in relation to its own values and objectives and in relation to those which may be wished on it by others. We shall look at its implications for higher education itself and at the reaction that can be expected from different parts of the higher-education system. We shall also try to consider the interests and expectations of the clients of Access courses and how far these are being met.

Ideologies of admissions

The Access-course movement is about much more than who should be admitted to higher education. But that provides our starting point: the organization of the admissions process. Fulton has recently drawn attention to two key characteristics of the approach to admissions in UK higher education: *competition* for places and *selection* – by *academics*, the future teachers of those they select (Fulton 1988). As Fulton points out, these are distinctive characteristics of the British 'extended élite' system of higher education. They have implications for the ways in which academics see the admissions process.

Within higher education at least four 'ideologies' of admissions can be discerned. The first and perhaps most commonly found of these connects admissions to the *quality and reputation* of departments and institutions. The ability to attract 'good' students has been seen as an indicator of a department's or institution's standing and reputation and of the quality of work undertaken within it. A-level-point scores have been used as standardized proxy measures of the quality of student intake. Thus the setting of the level of conditional offers is an act of some political significance, reinforced in recent years by the approach of the University Grants Committee (UGC) to performance indicators. As Fulton and Ellwood make clear in Chapter 3, admissions tutors in much of higher education acknowledge this approach as a major constituent in their behaviour, and many of them adhere to the value system underpinning it.

A second and related approach to admissions places the emphasis on *equity*. The concern here is that the competition for places is fair. From this perspective, admission to higher education is seen as a reward for ability and diligence. As with the quality and reputation ideology, A levels as a standard objective measure are central to the operation of the equity model. Students who have worked hard and have achieved good results 'deserve' to be rewarded by the offer of a place. Other 'non-standard' routes into higher education are suspect precisely because they rest on unstandardized measures of ability and attainment. Again, as Chapter 3 shows, the perception that this is a view held by parents, schools and the public at large conditions admissions tutors' practice.

For adherents to these first two ideologies of admissions, any movement away from universalistic criteria as represented by A-level scores creates problems. For the reputational, there is the problem of what students without A levels are going to count as in a quality ranking. For the equity, there is concern that some people have gained the prize of entry to higher education without taking part in the contest. Both positions find problems with any kind of non-standard entry, not just Access courses, but they do not depend on assumptions about lack of potential or ability of students so admitted. The problem is with the way in which potential and ability are proven. To put it another way, adherents of this position would question the grounds on which students with 'good' A-level passes are excluded from entry to courses in favour of 'non-standard' entrants.

The third and fourth ideologies of admissions have no problems with such considerations. What we might call the *social-engineering* approach shares with the equity model a concern about equality of opportunity. Where it differs is in its perception of the competition for places in higher education through progression through secondary education as intrinsically unfair. Therefore, a modification of the 'rules' of the entry competition to favour those disadvantaged by the standard A-level criteria is welcomed. Such concerns in many cases relate to broader political agendas which see social and occupational mobility through education as an important contribution towards achieving a fairer society. Thus, in looking at routes into higher education and the composition of students admitted, there is likely to be great concern with the social composition of the student group in terms of social class, ethnicity, gender and age. Thus, whereas the reputational ideology lays great store by the A-level-point scores of the student body, the social engineering ideology looks for a desired social composition. These positions represent ideological extremes. Advocates of an equity approach are less concerned about the composition of the student body providing that the students 'deserve' to be there.

The fourth approach to admissions can scarcely be regarded as ideological at all. It is best described as the *shortage-of-students* approach. Admissions tutors who have difficulty in filling places with conventionally qualified students may well be willing to look elsewhere, particularly if they belong to unfavoured subjects in low-status institutions. Where professional and institutional survival depends upon 'getting students', other ideological considerations are likely to take second place. It should be emphasized that shortage of students does not of itself lead to a liberal admissions policy. In a strong and prestigious institution where A-level-point scores are an important measure of departmental reputation and success, it may be politically more expedient to have empty places than to lower the A-level entry requirement.

As the above discussion has hinted, the admission process within higher-education institutions is a mixture of ideology and pragmatism. Although the 'pure' types sketched out above can be found throughout the system, a departmental or institutionally dominant approach is likely to be strongly influenced by institutional circumstances. Thus, concern about A-level-point scores as an indicator of quality and reputation is likely to be at its highest in institutions which attract 'good' A-level students. A policy of preferring non-standard entrants over applicants with 'poor' A levels may be more easily implemented than one which discriminates against 'good' A-level performance.

These contrasting approaches to admissions in higher education are relevant to a discussion about access courses because the debate about Access courses has been essentially an ideological one. The debate has brought out strong, if shifting and frequently confused, statements by government but it has also been the subject of intense debate within higher-education institutions. Admissions policy, like assessment policy, is a subject on which academic tempers seem frequently to fray.

Political supports and misgivings

The admission of mature students without the conventional entry qualifications is nothing new to higher education. It was given a boost in the mid-1970s when the grant regulations were changed to make such students eligible to receive mandatory awards. Previously eligibility for a grant was dependent upon the discretion of the local education authority. A small number of Access courses already existed at the time, some based in further-education colleges, a few in polytechnics. But the numbers involved were very small. The admission of students without conventional A-level qualifications on an exceptional basis was nevertheless quite widely practised, particularly in public-sector institutions. It usually involved exceptionally motivated mature students who had some qualifications (perhaps one A level) but who did not meet the minimum entrance requirements. Though lacking formal entry qualifications, such exceptional entrants were not socially and educationally disadvantaged in other ways. They were generally white and middle-class, though frequently female. Few courses admitted more than two to three such students in any one year, partly because the demand for places was not great from students of this sort (there was very little publicity given to the opportunities available) and, in the case of Council for National Academic Awards (CNAA) degree courses, because CNAA subject boards insisted that the proportions of exceptional entrants should be small.

The first political impetus to the development of Access courses came with an invitation from the Department of Education and Science (DES) in August 1978 to seven local education authorities to set up special courses for people who had 'special needs which cannot be met by existing educational arrangements' and who possessed 'valuable experience but lack the qualifications required' (Department of Education and Science 1978b). The courses were to prepare students for entry to higher education. They were to be evaluated to enable the DES to decide whether to encourage an extension in the provision of such courses.

Evidence that the DES initiative lay firmly in the 'social engineering' approach to admissions was provided by the Minister of State in a parliamentary answer which saw access courses

> as a contribution towards the policy of ensuring that all members of the community, including those from ethnic minority groups, have equal opportunities to develop their aptitudes and abilities to the full and, in particular, to undertake responsible careers which bring them into contact with the community.
>
> (Department of Education and Science 1978a)

The last point was given great prominence by several of the participating local authorities which saw Access courses as providing a mechanism for the recruitment and training of black professionals for jobs in teaching and social work in their own ethnic-minority communities. It is worth noting that three-quarters of the Access courses set up as a result of the DES initiative were in colleges of the Inner London Education Authority (ILEA) where this emphasis was given strong support.

Impetus to the Access-courses movement was provided by the inner-city troubles in the early 1980s and the attention which they focused upon the black communities. At the same time the incoming Conservative government of 1979 brought with it a different set of concerns about higher education. Two aspects of government policy towards higher education in the first Thatcher administration had particular importance for the Access-courses movement. One of these stemmed from the interests of the Secretary of State, Sir Keith Joseph, in standards of teaching and learning and in the curriculum which culminated in the setting up of the Lindop inquiry into validation in public-sector higher education. The second was the stringency of the financial cuts imposed upon higher education and the reaction, particularly that of the University Grants Committee, to them.

The questions posed by the Secretary of State brought higher-education admissions policy firmly back into the 'quality and reputation' agenda. A whole succession of government contributions to the access debate counselled caution in order to preserve standards. Thus the 1985 Green Paper welcomed Access courses with the important proviso that

> The challenge of non-standard entry is to maintain a reasonable degree of openness for late developers, and for those who for whatever reason did not enter higher education earlier, *while ensuring that academic rigour and standards are maintained.* [My emphasis]
> (Department of Education and Science 1985)

The implications of these reservations were taken up from the point of view of the Inspectorate. HMI Bolton wrote in the *Journal of Access Studies* that 'There is a price to be paid for more open access if the quality of the higher qualification is to be maintained and be of value to the student' (Bolton 1986).

He went on to suggest that

> Where a large proportion of students have little experience of academic study, or none at all, it is likely to take longer to reach higher education standards than it is when the majority of students have entered higher education via the traditional school/A-level route.

This emphasis upon *proportions* of 'non-standard' entrants was taken up by CNAA subject boards at around this time when several degree courses were limited to quotas of 'exceptional' entrants of around ten per cent of their total intake.

An influential contribution to the 'quality' debate on access came in the publication of the Lindop Report in 1985. First, the Lindop Report expressed support for the view that A-level-point scores did in fact indicate academic quality and that large variations in the scores required for entry into different institutions raise questions of comparability of standards between institutions and sectors. Although the Committee found no cause for concern about standards in public-sector higher education, it did nevertheless ask institutions and validating bodies to 'review procedures' in order to 'avoid the risk of problems'.

The Lindop Report counselled caution in three areas. One was the relationship between the 'receiving' higher-education institution and the 'providing' further-education institution. If this was too close, the result, according to the Committee, could be 'the formation of relationships and understandings which lead to students from the Access courses being accepted for degree courses even if they lack the ability to reach degree standard'. (Lindop Report 1985: 70) The second area of concern resulted in a call from the Committee for all institutions to have formal procedures for assessing applicants for degree courses who did not possess normal entry requirements. The third area of concern was in the proportions admitted: 'If too high a proportion of students is accepted for courses not designed for them they may founder and staff may be tempted to lower standards' (Lindop Report 1985: 71).

Quality concerns about access were linked with the funding crisis in higher education. Cuts, real and threatened, were high on the agenda in both sectors of higher education and indicators of institutional and course quality acquired a heightened significance in such circumstances. The currency of A-level-point scores remained strong and the question of how access students affected the calculation of the score was never really answered in most institutions of higher education.

Thus, despite the 1978 initiative, Access courses proved to be politically sensitive, inside and outside higher-education institutions. Messages from outside were contradictory. Thus, staff in London polytechnics were under pressure to respond to the enthusiastic access policies of the ILEA while fearing that someone at the DES was counting up their A-level-point scores.

The 1987 White Paper and subsequent government pronouncements have placed increasing emphasis on extending access and have seen Access courses as playing an important role in so doing. However, the emphasis has not been on higher-education admissions as providing 'social engineering', but on response to the more pragmatic concern about 'shortage of students' with conventional A-level qualifications in the early 1990s. The economic need for highly qualified manpower requires students to be found from other sources.

The White Paper referred to Access courses as providing a 'third route' into higher education. (The first route was A levels or their Scottish equivalents; the second route was vocational qualifications.) The closest that the White Paper got to linking Access courses to the repair of social and educational disadvantage was in asserting the importance of increasing the number of mature students. The government admitted that admissions through Access courses did not impair standards in higher education. However, there were clearly still political sensitivities on this score and the White Paper set out a number of requirements if 'risk to quality' was to be avoided. The government's requirements were that

(i) institutions providing Access courses must ensure that their content and method are well aligned to those of the higher education courses to which they lead;

(ii) institutions receiving students from Access courses must select students responsibly, taking advantage of the predictive value of their performance at access level and weighing the evidence of their commitment to learn;

(iii) all institutions involved must put effort into counselling students and supporting their motivation.

(Department of Education and Science 1987)

Several other national organizations began to express interest in the extension of access to higher education. Industry Matters, an initiative of the Royal Society of Arts, put the case for extending access this way: 'unless access is widened, employers, and the country as a whole, will be denied the supply of skills and competencies necessary for survival in a competitive world' (Industry Matters 1988). It also pointed to a 'pool of ability' among those currently denied admission to higher education and expressed concern about the distorting effect on the school curriculum of the emphasis given to A-level requirements.

The growing interest in extending access to higher education by bodies outside it has given both impetus and greater respectability to the Access courses movement. The CNAA has responded to an invitation from the DES to establish a national framework for the recognition of access courses. The invitation reflects the importance which the DES now attaches to the 'third route' of entry into higher education. The establishment of the national framework represents an attempt to impose some order on to the four hundred or so separate Access-course initiatives. As such, it might eventually become a means of ensuring some element of standardization and universalism to the Access-courses movement, thereby addressing some of the concerns of the *quality* and *equity* lobbies within higher education.

The Access-courses movement

So far we have looked at Access courses from the outside. We have looked at the policy contexts which gave rise to and constrained them. We have looked at the different ideologies of admissions that can be found within higher-education institutions and their implications for different forms of access. The proponents of access courses themselves seem almost universally to belong to the *social engineering* approach to admissions. It is a radical movement in the sense that it sees education as a means by which whole social groups can improve their social, economic and political positions within British society. It is also radical in an educational sense. The social groups which represent the primary clients of Access courses are seen to have been 'failed' by the conventional educational system. The Access-course movement is founded on a rejection of such failure and of the criteria which have defined it. It has developed a conception of education that builds upon and fully recognizes the cultures of the client groups. Thus access courses are not 'watered down' A levels. To quite a great extent they reject the educational assumptions on which A levels are based. But in rejecting the culture of A levels, they pose major challenges for the culture of higher education itself.

It is dangerous to imply that there is a single unifying approach to the development of access courses among the hundreds of staff in further- and higher-education institutions who have been associated with them. However, some of the essential features are contained in the following quotation:

> Access Courses are designed jointly by higher education and further education institutions to enable adults to bridge the gap between their particular experiences and skills and the requirements of a degree course. Though developed mainly in response to the needs of mature students (and often of particular groups of mature students), they have become increasingly associated with the view that courses should be student-based rather than syllabus- or institution-based, and with the growing conviction that A-levels are neither a necessarily accurate measure of undergraduate potential, nor a particularly suitable preparation for undergraduate study.
>
> (Woodrow 1986)

A more radical formulation would pay much greater attention to the potential of access courses to bring about social change. Thus Lieven has written about the hope that higher-education expansion might help break down social-class barriers and create a more equal society. Access courses offered 'at least the possibility of significantly altering the class basis of higher education' (Lieven 1988: 65). Lieven also draws out the radical implications for the higher-education curriculum. The culture of higher education is seen by Lieven as 'predominantly that of the white, male, professional academy' and applauds access courses for placing 'black writers, women's issues, local history and the economy, the environment and the third world . . . in the forefront of the curriculum' (ibid., 65).

Less contentious features of Access courses have been the attention given to the development of study skills and the greater use made of the student's own experience. However, the latter has almost inevitably pushed at the boundaries of what counts as educational knowledge.

The majority of Access courses have had outlets in particular degree courses and therefore a much closer 'matching' of requirements has been possible than is found in the national system of A levels. The collaboration between staff in further and higher education has been widely seen as a factor behind the success of Access courses. However, as we have seen in the case of the Lindop Report, it has been a cause of concern for some and it has limited the range of higher-education opportunities open to access students.

The successful collaboration between further- and higher-education staff has not prevented conflicts within the receiving higher-education institutions where other teaching staff have not always been as enthusiastic as their colleagues for the educational philosophies of Access courses. The extent and nature of conflict have depended in part on the subject area of study. Where degree courses, especially in the sciences, have traditionally assumed the possession of a substantial amount of subject-specific knowledge among first-year students, it has been more difficult to make the access-course philosophy work. Thus, in a recent study, Osborne and Woodrow found science access courses placing greater emphasis upon knowledge content than skills and taking a discipline-based approach rather than a student-centred one. The researchers found some reluctance on the part of higher-education staff to respond to newer approaches to learning (Osborne and Woodrow in press).

Where the cultures of further and higher education have been close, higher education has more easily been able to relate to the ideology of Access courses. However, discipline-centred research-oriented academics are less prepared to negotiate the curriculum. Mature and other non-traditional students may be welcomed but the need for adjustment is seen to lie with the students, not with the staff. In some fields, professional-body requirements provide a further constraint on the higher-education curriculum.

The desirability of modifying the nature and content of higher education to accommodate access students more easily is, of course, strongly contested. The approach to learning and to knowledge adopted by access courses is for some a 'superior' approach which should be taken up across all higher education. For others the modification of curriculum and pedagogy would deny to access students the rewards of a 'proper' discipline-based higher education.

The success of Access courses

The evaluation report of the Access courses set up in response to the 1978 DES initiative was concerned with 36 courses running in 1983/4, a figure which had built up from the 11 courses running in the selected LEAs when the project started in 1979. A total of 2023 students took the courses between 1979 and 1983.

The scale of the Access-courses movement has expanded enormously over the last decade. There are estimated to be around four hundred courses now on offer. Given this rate of expansion, it can only be surmised how representative the findings of the 1984 evaluation report are for this expanded Access-course provision. However, with that important reservation in mind, its main findings are worth recording.

The proportion of courses offered by the ILEA was between 73 per cent and 81 per cent of the total, varying according to the year in question. This must partially account for the composition of the student body. Students of Caribbean origins accounted for 51 per cent and white British 37 per cent.

There were very few students from other ethnic groups. Over 60 per cent of the students were below 30; 72 per cent were women; 67 per cent successfully completed their Access courses and of these 94 per cent went on to higher education, 82 per cent to a linked course in a partner higher-education institution. In the early years courses geared to teaching and employment in the social services accounted for 40 per cent of the students. Later years saw the introduction of Access courses preparing students for degree courses in sciences, engineering and business studies. Of the first cohort of Access course students 71 per cent successfully completed their degree courses (Millins 1984). The report concluded that there was sufficient evidence to justify the DES's encouraging the development of still more Access courses.

A more recent study of Access courses in mathematics, science and technology (Osborne and Woodrow in press) found an ethnic composition which was 51.5 per cent white European, 23 per cent Caribbean, 15 per cent African and 7 per cent Asian. The low proportion of Asian students on Access courses needs to be seen in the context of the quite high proportion of Asian students entering higher education with conventional school-leaving qualifications (Brennan and McGeevor 1987). The success rates on the maths and science Access courses studied by Osborne and Woodrow were only slightly lower than those reported in the earlier study by Millins; 60 per cent of the students passed the Access courses, almost all of whom progressed on to higher education, 44 per cent into linked higher-education institutions and 15 per cent into non-linked institutions.

One particular conclusion of the Osborne and Woodrow study is worth highlighting. They report that assessment methods in many Access courses are weighted towards the assessment procedures of higher education with between 40 per cent and 60 per cent of total marks devoted to unseen examinations. Feedback from students indicated that substantial numbers felt ill prepared for taking such examinations. This points to one of the main dilemmas for staff designing access courses: how far to confront the students with those 'traditional' features of secondary and higher examinations that are alien to such students and which may be associated with their earlier educational failure? Too great a contrast between the educational cultures of Access courses and degree courses runs the risk of adjustment problems and the danger of failure on the degree course. Yet Access courses which fail to recognize the special needs of their clientele will themselves not be successful. The answer to the problem may ultimately point to the need for change in the design and content of degree courses themselves. (This point is taken up further in succeeding chapters of this book, especially Chapters 5, 6 and 8.)

Standardization or diversity?

In its recently revised degree-course regulations, the CNAA has removed the distinction long made between standard and non-standard entrants. In so doing it has recognized the increasing heterogeneity of qualifications which can lead to entry into higher education. However, the question which this raises is whether within this heterogeneity a common standard can be discerned, both in terms of general educational levels of attainment and of subject-specific knowledge and skills. What should designers and teachers of degree courses assume to be the starting point of their first-year students? Many courses already recruit heterogeneous intakes but many do not. What is the incentive to persuade the latter to broaden their intakes?

The answer to this question is sometimes given in terms of demographic change and the predicted shortfall of conventionally qualified 18-year-olds. Even if the predictions are correct, demography is unlikely to provide a wholly satisfactory answer. The more prestigious institutions and subjects in high demand will not face a shortage of students. If reputational and equity concerns continue to support an emphasis on standardized admissions procedures, with A levels remaining the only standardized measure, then most admissions tutors can continue to ignore the expanding but 'messy' end of the admissions market.

Would this matter? The success of the local links between further-education courses and degree courses in the public sector should not blind us to their limitations. The educational opportunities open to the successful student from an Access course are severely restricted compared with those open to an A-level student. And not just educational opportunities. The chances of getting a good degree and, beyond that, a good job are generally lower for students entering public-sector institutions (Boys and Kirkland 1988; Council for National Academic Awards 1988). Without taking account of sector differences, the employment opportunities for graduates from ethnic minorities are much less than for their white counterparts (Brennan and McGeevor, op. cit.). The more degree courses in the polytechnics and colleges are adapted to cater for new kinds of students without a comparable adaptation of university courses, the greater the sectoral disparity of educational and employment outcomes is likely to be in the future.

The national framework for the recognition of Access courses being set up by the CNAA, in collaboration with the Committee of Vice-Chancellors and Principals, is likely to have a major bearing on the opportunities open to students from such courses. It should certainly broaden the range of outlets for students from particular Access courses. But how far will it persuade admissions tutors on courses where reputation and quality concerns are paramount that access students are 'good' students? How far will Access courses distinguish their most capable students? Rankings along the lines of A-level scores run counter to the ideology of Access courses. Without such rankings, will Access-course students have the opportunities available to the A-level student with good grades?

The old tripartite system of secondary education was a system characterized as providing 'sponsored' mobility for pupils selected for secondary school at the age of eleven (Turner 1960). The removal of selection was meant to promote a fairer 'contest' by keeping opportunities open to a much later stage. The growth of access courses and the problems of educational disadvantage which they are meant to address reflect the failure to keep the contest open. Access courses provide a 'second chance' for people that have been failed by the earlier stages of education. They can be justified on grounds of equity precisely because of the lack of fairness in the earlier contest. But the attainment of their objectives requires education institutions to get involved in social engineering to an extent that some may be reluctant to contemplate.

One of the last acts of the National Advisory Body was the publication of the report of its Equal Opportunities Group entitled *Action for Access*. The report comes out unambiguously in favour of greater equality of opportunity in higher education and proposes a programme of positive action to achieve it. The report received only lukewarm support from government and its crucial funding proposals were not accepted by its successor body, the Polytechnics and Colleges Funding Council. The removal of the LEA presence in the national funding body and the breaking of the LEA–institution link at the local level are unlikely to reverse the expansion of the Access-courses movement. But they do raise questions about how far its ultimate goal will remain the achievement of equality of opportunity and how far it is being converted into a strategy primarily concerned with meeting economic demand during a period of a shortfall of 'conventional' students. The answers will determine the permanence and the extensiveness of the changes that higher-education institutions will need to make in response to the challenge of the Access-courses movement.

References

Bolton, E. (1986) 'Quality issues arising from expanding access', *Journal of Access Studies*, 1 (1).

Boys, C. and Kirkland, J. (1988) *Degrees of Success*, London, Jessica Kingsley Publishers.

Brennan, J. L. and McGeevor, P. A. (1987) *The Employment of Graduates from Ethnic Minorities*, London, Commission for Racial Equality.

Council for National Academic Awards (1988) *Degree Results and Employment Destinations in the Social Sciences*, Outcomes Paper 1, London, Council for National Academic Awards.

Council for National Academic Awards (1989) *Access Courses to Higher Education*, London, Council for National Academic Awards.

Department of Education and Science (1978a) *Special Courses in Preparation for Entry to Higher Education*, press notice, London, Department of Education and Science.

Department of Education and Science (1978b) *Special Courses in Preparation for Entry to Higher Education*, letter of invitation to Chief Education Officers, London, Department of Education and Science.

Department of Education and Science (1985) *The Development of Higher Education into the 1990s*, Cmnd 9524, London, HMSO.

Department of Education and Science (1987) *Higher Education: Meeting the Challenge*, Cm. 114, London, HMSO.

Fulton, O. (1988) 'Elite survivals? Entry "standards" and procedures for higher education admissions', *Studies in Higher Education*, 13 (1).

Heron, G. (1986) 'Access, quality, community', *Journal of Access Studies*, 1 (2).

Industry Matters (1987) *Raising the Standard: Wider Access to Higher Education*, London, Industry Matters.

Lieven, M. (1988) 'The liberal progressive movement and access to higher education', *Higher Education Review*, 20 (3).

Lindop Report (1985) *Academic Validation in Public Sector Higher Education*, Cmnd 9501, London, HMSO.

Millins, P. K. C. (1984) *Access Studies to Higher Education (September 1979–December 1983): a Report*, Roehampton, Roehampton Institute.

Millins, P. K. C. (1986) 'Access and quality control: the Lindop onslaught', *Journal of Access Studies*, 1 (2).

National Advisory Body (1988) *Action for Access: Widening Opportunities in Higher Education*, London, National Advisory Body for Public Sector Higher Education.

Osborne, M. and Woodrow, M. (in press) *Access to Mathematics, Science and Technology*, Project report to Further Education Unit, London, Further Education Unit.

Turner, R. H. (1960) 'Sponsored and contest mobility and the school system', *American Sociological Review*, 25 (1).

Woodrow, M. (1986) 'Scrutiny in partnership: access issues from eighteen courses in South London', *Journal of Access Studies*, 1 (1).

5

Qualification, Paradigms and Experiential Learning in Higher Education

Robin Usher

Prior experiential learning is increasingly being seen as an appropriate qualification for higher education and an alternative to traditional A-level qualifications. This development, in creating an alternative admission route, clearly benefits the potential adult student and thus opens up the possibility of a significant widening of access to higher education.

Two related themes will be explored in this chapter. The first concerns the implications of this development for our understanding of being 'qualified' for higher education. The demand for the assessment of prior experiential learning is gradually creating systematized procedures designed to establish its credibility as an alternative qualification. These procedures will be critically examined.

The second concerns the relationship between qualifications, standards and boundaries. The assumption is that being qualified only makes sense in relation to a standard which sets boundaries and maintains exclusivity. Standards and boundaries are paradigmatically located so our current understanding of being 'qualified' must be seen in terms of a dominant knowledge paradigm within higher education which, however, is increasingly under pressure and therefore open to change.

Paradigm change and the emphasis on prior experiential learning mutually influence one another and produce the possibility of widening access to higher education. However, there are dangers that in allowing the process of assessing experiential learning to become too mechanistic, regulatory pressures will reassert their dominance over the reform of higher education. Consequently, the chance for a more open and flexible interpretation of qualification, which is both a cause and an effect of widening access, will be lost.

Experiential learning and access to higher education

Experiential learning can be defined as: 'the knowledge and skills acquired through life and work experience and study which are not formally attested through any educational or professional certification' (Evans 1983: 3). The justification normally given for thus using experiential learning is based on the assumption that people have learnt and continue to learn through their life and work experience. They bring this learning with them to higher education and therefore it can be recognized through appropriate assessment. This involves systematizing it in terms of specific knowledge and skills, a process that is thought to require reflection. In effect, the raw material of subjective experience is transformed into 'objective' statements of learning outcomes.

Clearly, adults seeking access to higher education undoubtedly possess experience, greater both in quantity and variety than that of the average school-leaver. In this sense experience has always been 'recognized' as a useful indicator of maturity, positive motivation and serious study intentions. It gave selectors an informal guide to the existence of desirable attitudinal and behavioural qualities which, in some respects, could be considered to compensate for the lack of the theoretical background knowledge and study skills supposedly conferred by formal qualifications. Of course, the inevitable consequence was a very narrow access route for potential adult students. Experience on its own was never considered enough and, even when taken into account, those who successfully squeezed through have always been the exceptional few. Very often, experience was ignored on the grounds that it was a poor indicator of intellectual and academic aptitude. It is clear, however, that experience, whether recognized as useful or not, tended to be seen in an *undifferentiated* way.

Sweden was probably the first country to develop a systematic, national policy designed to widen access to higher education by making experience the norm rather than the exception for entry, through the 25/4 rule which emphasized the *duration* of experience. The *nature* of the experience was not prescribed nor was any attempt made to relate particular kinds of experience to particular kinds of study.

The 25/4 rule was part of a wide-ranging reform of higher education designed to further certain social and economic aims. Enabling adults to enter higher education was intended to promote both inter- and intra-generational equality and the development of appropriately skilled manpower through the opportunity for retraining and updating.

The reforms were therefore not primarily educational in intent, although educational aims were implicit. Consequently, access policy, as defined by the 25/4 rule, could be broad in scope and flexible in operation, enabling a large-scale opening of the doors of higher education for those hitherto excluded. By not getting too enmeshed in the details of experience and its relationship to particular kinds of studies, the application of the broad 25/4 rule did not erect new barriers to access and therefore led to clear, positive macro-consequences.

However, evidence indicates that adult students so admitted felt they had inadequate theoretical background knowledge and deficient study skills, and experienced difficulty coping (Dahlgren and Marton 1978; Kim 1982). Whilst experience may be a learning resource, the confidence to use it is not always present. Widening access through adopting a broad and flexible rule emphasizing undifferentiated experience may thus lead to questionable educational consequences. If adult students are thought to be unable to cope, this arouses fears of high failure and drop-out rates. The emphasis has therefore shifted from undifferentiated experience to the *learning* derived from experience. The idea now is that access can be widened by recognizing not *experience* but prior *experiential learning*. This 'accredited' learning can then function as an equivalent to formal qualifications.

It was this argument which led me in an earlier analysis (Usher 1986) to highlight the role of reflection in providing the vital link between experience and its learning outcomes. Reflection was also seen as a learning process involving the skills and knowledge needed for being a successful student in higher education.

For access, therefore, experience as an alternative to formal qualifications is thought to require systematic and 'objective' evidence that experience has been subjected to reflection. This seems to present clear advantages both for adults seeking non-traditional entry and for selectors assessing their suitability. As a result, socio-economic and educational considerations might actually be reconcilable.

In the last few years, the movement to 'accredit' prior experiential learning has gathered pace and momentum and the literature relating to its theory and practice has undergone considerable expansion. But concepts such as 'experience', 'reflection', 'competency' and 'learning' and the operating procedures of APEL (Accredition of Prior Experiential Learning) are in need of examination. My standpoint in doing this is an acceptance, first, that widening access to higher education by opening the doors to non-traditional adult students is both desirable and necessary and, second, that bringing this about is bound to involve major changes over time in institutions of higher education.

A changing paradigm of adult abilities and its consequences

First, however, it is necessary to examine briefly the background of recent developments in the way in which adults themselves have been theorized. These developments are based on the cognitive science paradigm and the research it has generated. The suggestion is that adults through the course of their lives construct specialized knowledge within specific domains, an expertise consisting of highly developed situational understanding.

Expert knowledge within specific domains is not 'hard-wired' but self-constructed and accessible to self-awareness. It depends on experience and motivation and develops through use. Problem-solving, for example, draws on skills and knowledge specific to a domain rather than central, componential abilities.

Allied to this are developments in our understanding of post-formal thinking. Perry (1968) illustrated the development of relativistic and contextual thinking. Sinnott (1984) has shown that adults use relativistic thinking in solving real-life problems. Rybash *et al.* (1986: 82) comment that:

> with increasing age adults display an increased awareness of relativity, an acceptance of contradiction as a basic aspect of reality and an ability to synthesize contradictions into higher order wholes.

In post-formal thinking knowledge is viewed as relative, perspective dependent and constructed by individuals rather than merely reflecting a fixed external reality. Frameworks of understanding are open rather than closed. The emphasis is on integration and synthesis rather than differentiation and compartmentalization.

Adulthood, therefore, is characterized by a movement from novice to expert through the construction of specialized domain-specific knowledge which is experientially based, contextually oriented and used relativistically and critically. Adults, because of their experience, can be knowledge constructors and can think in complex ways.

This picture is clearly useful in backing up the claim that adults have both the ability and the aptitude to cope generally with higher education. There is an optimism which contrasts sharply with earlier maturational theorizations which stressed inevitable and irreversible cognitive decline and certainly did not recognize that even 'ordinary' adults could possess a fund of specialized knowledge and might actually be able to think and reason in really quite sophisticated ways. More specifically, this optimism appears both to warrant and facilitate the development of approaches for credentialling prior experiential learning.

This theorization of adulthood is part of a new, developing paradigm, opposed to the maturational paradigm of cognitive decline. Now, it seems, decline is not inevitable. How has this new paradigm gained credibility and acceptability?

Paradigms have to be seen as part of a network of practices within the discipline of psychology, the education system and the wider society in which all are located. The maturational paradigm was a vital component in a network which privileged children and 'front-end' schooling and marginalized the provision of educational opportunities for adults. Marginalization was itself the product of a socio-economic situation where no powerful motive existed for extending educational opportunities beyond a certain age.

Maturational theorizations took central processes and componential abilities as objects of enquiry and psychometric testing as the preferred mode of research. Models of adult development were therefore constructed on this basis with biography and context ignored or downgraded. The consequence was that education for adults other than of a purely leisure or recreational kind was seen as largely pointless on any large scale. Psychological theorizations and perceived socio-economic needs came together to produce both an educational policy that neglected post-compulsory education and a marginalized provision that assigned adults a low priority.

With the change in paradigm a different and more 'liberating' picture emerges. Cognitive decline is no longer inevitable since central processes and componential abilities are not taken as key factors in cognitive effectiveness in the 'real' world. Naturalistic modes of research replace laboratory experimentation and testing and new theoretical models which more 'authentically' capture adult development are constructed. Adults are therefore *constituted* differently by being accorded a capacity for lifelong development and by being attributed experiential, expert knowledge and advanced powers of reasoning. If experience counts, then adults are no longer 'bad bets' and therefore 'deserve' a higher priority educationally.

Equally, however, there have been significant changes in perceived socio-economic needs. The backdrop to these changes is a demographic trend implying a twenty-five per cent fall in the number of school-leavers in the next ten years.

The consequences of this trend are interestingly (and in my view paradigmatically) sketched out by the Training Commission.[1] They argue that, since there will be fewer young people, they will be difficult to recruit and hence more expensive. Second, since young people can no longer be drawn upon to replace adults with out-of-date skills, the latter will need updating through education and training. Third, as products, services and technology change, so adults will have to be developed for new roles.

I have highlighted this not because I want to dispute the accuracy of the forecasts, but because of the way it is being *interpreted*. This interpretation is part of the paradigm shift which through a changing theorization of adulthood is 'strengthening' the case for increased educational and especially training opportunities and provision for adults. But the shift, although encouraging educational reform and increased opportunity, is not purely 'liberating'. The arguments made by the Training Commission exemplify the regulatory factors that also exist.

Earlier I made the point that, in the heyday of the maturational paradigm, no powerful motive existed for extending educational opportunities for adults beyond a certain age. In effect, no powerful *regulatory* motive existed, since any regulation of adults could be readily achieved in sites and through practices other than the educational. Now, however, regulatory practices which involve the 'formation' of adults in skills and attitudes perceived as functional to the current and evolving socio-economic structure are already with us and likely to increase. Adults have joined children and young people as significant objects both of psychological theorization and research and of educational and training practices whose purpose is increasingly regulatory.

There are two implications that can be drawn from all this. The first is that the demand for higher education by adults without formal entry qualifications has to a very large extent been *created*. Let me explain this rather controversial statement. It is not that the demand is somehow not 'real' but it is crucially dependent on the paradigm shift I have described. Once that shift has started, then attitudes begin to change – the unthinkable becomes the thinkable, the immutable becomes the conventional and thus open to the possibility of change, the system that appeared to be working now no longer seems to do so. The door hitherto perceived by adults as closed seems to be slowly opening, and not having formal qualifications now no longer seems the terminus of hopes and aspirations. When the impossible becomes the possible, demand which is latent and ignored becomes manifest and recognized.

The second implication concerns the regulatory aspects mentioned above. Currently we are at the stage where widening access to higher education for non-traditional students is considered a 'good thing' by both educationalists and government. The former couch their arguments in the liberal ideology of equality of opportunity, the individual's right to lifelong education, the need to develop talent and potential – all the arguments, in other words, which educationalists traditionally use in trying to change a system which is already beginning to move. The government argues for more highly trained 'manpower' and responding to the 'complex needs' of a changing society.[2] So far, both educationalists and government, whatever else their differences, are at one on the need to widen access.

But this 'liberating' discourse disguises a subtle shift in emphasis, best exemplified by the Training Commission arguments noted earlier. These have a familiar ring – skill shortages, costs, pools of labour, updating, preparation for new roles. My purpose in highlighting this is not to comment specifically on the merits of these arguments but to make the point that their emphasis is functional, instrumental and therefore regulatory. We are no longer in the realm of educational reform guided solely by educational criteria. The 'good thing' is about to be overtaken by the functionally necessary. Something that has the potential for empowerment is about to be incorporated.

Of course, it could be rightly argued that no educational reform is ever autonomous but is always interwoven with the state's perceived need for social control, particularly in view of the intimate connection of education with power. On the other hand, this makes it even more necessary for educators to adopt a problematizing stance towards educational changes which can so easily become mere instruments for social control rather than means for empowerment.

Specifically there is a danger that, despite sincere attempts to make APEL a practical and facilitative reality for potential adult students, a regulatory mechanism could be entering through the backdoor. At the moment there is a crusading even Messianic flavour about what has rightly developed into a 'movement'. This is perhaps not surprising at this stage of development, given the difficulties that have been and will continue to be encountered. Currently the avowed purpose is empowerment but the structure being laid down, however useful, may unwittingly be moving rather towards control.

A critique of the APEL process and procedures

The APEL process and procedures will be examined through a representative text, *Assessing Experiential Learning* (Evans 1987). The assumption underlying the process is that 'hidden within all students whatever their age, aspirations or qualifications lies a mass of knowledge and skills acquired in a variety of ways' (para. 59).

Given this, the need is for a process enabling self-recognition and a context which will 'facilitate, encourage and support reflection on experience' (para. 61). Reflection, as I have noted earlier, is a key aspect since it is only learning outcomes that matter.

Although this seems reasonable enough, problems now begin to appear. The first arises from 'the possible tension between the essentially private activity of reflecting on experience and the public activity of having the learning from that activity assessed' (para. 62). The answer apparently is to recognize the 'personal ownership of experiential learning', a right which must remain 'inviolate'.

But, as soon as learning is put into the public domain, it ceases to be exclusively personal. Learning does not exist as a generalized phenomenon invariant across all contexts: 'the meaning of the concept of learning is thus to be sought in the socially and culturally established conventions with respect to what counts as learning in specific educational environments' (Saljo 1987: 104).

Institutions of higher education have such conventions and it is *their* definition of what counts as learning which is the operative one as far as the potential student is concerned. Whilst the latter could be rightfully said to own his/her *experience*, learning outcomes must inevitably be structured in relation to the external definition, otherwise there is no recognized equivalence with formal qualifications. The fact is that, for the potential adult student seeking non-formal admittance, it is not the case that any learning outcomes will do but only those judged as worthy in terms of the relevant intellectual demands.

There is a further point to be made here. In the process of assessing experiential learning four stages are recommended:

● systematic reflection on experience for significant learning.
● identification of significant learning, expressed in precise statements, constituting claims to the possession of knowledge and skills.
● synthesis of evidence to support the claims made to knowledge and skills.
● assessment for accreditation.

(Evans 1987, para. 70)

Apart from the fact that this in itself constitutes quite a formidable set of hurdles (a point I shall return to later), the staged procedure, indeed the whole process, is geared to the 'objectification' of learning for external assessment. With each stage of the process a greater distance is placed between the potential student and his/her learning until by the final assessment stage the distancing is such that the loss of personal control, a key aspect of ownership, is complete.

The next problem relates to a difficulty in the first and second stages. The procedure recommends:

sifting through personal experience for occasions when something was learnt. . . . Nothing need be excluded if it has led to some learning. . . . However some of the learning so identified will be obviously more relevant than other parts to the overall learning task in view.

(Evans 1987, para. 71)

No experience therefore must be excluded if it has led to some learning. But how is one to know in advance whether it has or not? Furthermore some learning is 'more relevant' but this, however, cannot be known in advance, otherwise there would be no point in going through the exercise. Yet it is this very learning which is also the criterion for judging ('sifting through') one's experience. In principle, to overcome this problem, *all* experience needs considering (apparently suggested by the recommendation that 'nothing need be excluded'). But this would be impossible both practically and in the sense that we never come naïve to our experience. First, our very conceptions of what constitutes experience are located in discursive paradigms which influence what we actually experience. Second, there is a circular hermeneutic relationship between experience, understanding and learning.

This implies that experience is not separable from one's life history; indeed the latter is the indispensable context within which one's experience unfolds. We understand ourselves and our lives through our experiences, whose significance changes with the development of our life history and the way we interpret it. In other words, we always learn about our experiences holistically. If experience is located in the unfolding of a holistic life history, then distancing one from the other by objectifying experience both distorts experience and restricts understanding.

We are told also that systematic reflection is the means by which a decision can be made as to whether a particular experience is 'significant' in terms of learning. This implies that reflection is a kind of mechanistic procedure (indeed the word 'tool' is actually used) whose application allows experience to be transformed into learning outcomes. Here we have yet another instance of the overpsychologizing of reflection (Kemmis 1985). If, however, we see reflection as influenced by interests in the Habermasian sense and by experience in the sense just described, then reflection as the process necessary for understanding is now part of the hermeneutic relationship. This suggests a complexity not easily encapsulated in a set of invariant, mechanistic procedures.

The third problem is to do with the notion of 'competences'. At the stage of 'identifying significant learning' it is clear that what is required is an articulation of learning outcomes in terms of the competences which have been reached, the matching of these with the competences thought to be required by the course and the assembling of evidence to substantiate the claimed competences.

The notion of competence is central to the APEL procedures (Gorringe 1987; Buckle 1988). Buckle defines it as: 'a blend of skills, knowledge, aptitudes and attitudes successfully applied, for example, to complete a task or achieve a demonstrable outcome' (p. 4).

The emphasis here is clearly on 'performance'. Potential students need to demonstrate what they know, how well they know it and at what level. Statements of competence level and quality, expressed through an appropriate terminology with performative examples, are therefore crucial. Simosko (1988) argues that statements of learning outcomes should:

● be unambiguous and readily understandable by both student and teacher
● describe observable, demonstrable and assessable performance
● contain action verbs which have relatively few meanings.

(p. 13)

If all this has a somewhat familiar ring, it is hardly surprising for it is, in effect, behavioural objectives revisited. Potential students are advised to couch their statements in terms of six levels of learning – knowledge of facts, interpretation of factual knowledge, application, analysis, synthesis and evaluation and give examples of what they can do using verbs such as 'list', 'specify', 'enumerate', 'appraise', etc. The six levels are in fact Bloom's taxonomy of educational objectives and its associated behavioural terminology.

Without embarking on a critique of behaviourism it is, however, important to emphasize the foundation of APEL in a behaviourist paradigm which does not appear to be explicitly stated in the literature, let alone problematized. Some comment is therefore in order.

First, since learning has to be stated in terms of 'unambiguous' performance statements, the assumption is that if one cannot do so, then no learning has taken place. But must learning always be performatively stable and demonstrable? Even at the most obvious level this seems unnecessarily restrictive. Second, why the emphasis on an 'appropriate' terminology of 'action verbs'? This could become a strait-jacket where finding the right word assumes the status of a ritual which must be gone through at the expense of the process of learning. The search for an *unambiguous* terminology seems a chimera too. What is ambiguous to one person may seem perfectly clear to another. All words have to be interpreted and their meaning resides not in explicit dictionary-type definition but in how they are used – and this itself depends on context, tradition and disposition.

There is a very real danger that in adopting such a behaviourist approach, emphasis is placed entirely on the end-product, the accrediting of learning outcomes rather than the process of learning itself. While it may rightly be claimed that ideally a balance is required, there is always a difficulty in striking this because of the tendency of product to overwhelm process. Getting the balance right requires careful consideration of questions such as who controls the procedures, who makes the decisions about what is required and what constitutes satisfactory evidence of competence (Bainbridge 1988). By emphasizing behaviouristic procedures these key questions are ignored.

The notion of competence is one which traditionally is related to competence-based training related to a specific job, X. The question in such training is always – what does the trainee need in order to do X? But what is X in the context of studies in higher education? What would constitute satisfactory evidence of competence? How are potential students to demonstrate competence when much of higher education does not itself generally know what competences are required for particular courses? This is not just a temporary inconvenience since for many courses predefined competences would anyhow be inappropriate.

One is not rejecting the notion of competence since this would itself be simplistic. But to make it the centrepiece of something that purportedly 'places students at the heart of the process', that is based on 'a developmental view of people as learners' and supposedly governed by a recognition of 'the characteristics of adults as learners' is odd to say the least. There certainly appears to be an incongruity which arises through uncritically locating a process which claims to be person-centred within a behaviourist paradigm which quite clearly is not.

The problem here is two-fold. First, the APEL procedures become 'techniques' the more they are systematized and codified. Techniques are, of course, instrumental and as such are clearly ambivalent in their effects. On the one hand, they can enable the effective achievement of given ends but, precisely because of this, their effect can also be that people are treated mechanistically – in other words, their subjectivity is made into an object that can be controlled and regulated.

Second, and related to this, experience has been reduced to raw material that can be transformed into a 'commodity' – assessed experiential learning – which can then be 'exchanged' for entrance and advanced standing. But in making it into a commodity that can be so exchanged, it is abstracted and objectified and is thus market-centred rather than person-centred.

Standards and boundaries

The fear of a dilution of academic standards is currently one of the major barriers to further progress in widening access. Existing admissions systems are based on A-level grades; standardization and consistency are the means for preserving academic standards. Whether they are a good predictor of final attainment or capacity to cope with studies has been considered less important.

In reality, adult students with non-traditional qualifications do no worse generally than students coming straight from school with A levels. But their actual number has been and continues to be too small for this kind of evidence to have much of an impact. None the less it does tend to reinforce the argument that the real purpose of A levels is not to select in but to select out. Any formal admission requirement is inevitably restrictive in selecting who is likely to be successful in attaining the exit standard. In this sense, A levels undoubtedly have the merit of ensuring 'standardization' but do so *because* they select out rather than select in.

The A level as the entry standard of higher education is actually a convention which has proved convenient for a higher-education system structured on élitist lines (see Chapters 2 and 3). If our system were different, then our present notions of academic entry and exit standards would be inappropriate. Equally, if our standards were different, so too would be our system. This is merely to point to the fact that standards are socially constructed rather than transcendentally given.

Equally, however, a standard is more than just a 'convention' because it is also a norm. It defines 'worthwhile' knowledge and appropriate capabilities, dispositions and behaviour. It creates boundaries which exclude and thus preserve the standard.[3] This constitutive power, however, has the appearance of a neutral and fair instrument for ensuring standardization and consistency.

Academic standards in higher education are part of a paradigmatic network of practices involving power and knowledge in an intimate and interactive relationship. Higher education is about the formation and distribution of 'worthwhile' knowledge. This knowledge creates, indeed *is*, power, because it can create 'difference' and enforce boundaries, defining who can legitimately possess it and who cannot. But power is itself maintained by the possession and monopolization of knowledge and the control through research over the means of creating and recreating it.

This suggests that academic standards are perhaps only the visible tip of the iceberg. The invisible part which forms a tradition in the Gadamerian sense is the conception that 'worthwhile' knowledge is objective, external, corresponds to the 'truth' of reality, is incrementally accumulated by methodical means and divisible into autonomous subjects or disciplines. It is hierarchically graded – boundaries within boundaries, exclusions within exclusions. The generation of new knowledge through pure research occupies a privileged position and is an important determinant of status, the distribution of resources and general attitudes and orientations. It contributes to exclusivity on the grounds of the need to maintain the highest 'standards' of research and relegates student-centred provision to a lower priority. Finally, the role of the teacher is that of the purveyor (the expert) who transmits knowledge to the student (the novice), thus ensuring a completely unequal power relationship.

Of course, I have painted an exaggerated picture to make my point. The higher-education system is not a monolith – the polytechnics, for example, emphasize applied rather than pure research and have been far more relaxed about drawing boundaries. Even within universities, which come closest to my portrayal, arts and social science have always deviated from the paradigm (which may perhaps suggest why mature students have flourished best there).

Equally, oppositional cultures challenging the dominant knowledge paradigm are not simply a recent phenomenon. But lately they have become less marginalized (the present publication could perhaps be seen as an example). Undoubtedly the paradigm is under challenge, beset by 'anomalies' which originate from contradictions within the higher-education system and by pressures from changing socio-economic structures. This might suggest that changing the paradigm and its network of associated practices and tradition would not be too difficult. After all, what is socially constructed can, in principle, be deconstructed and reconstructed.

Things, however, are never that simple. Practices and traditions may for some appear to be oppressive and outmoded but for others they still define what is worth while and thus what goals and purposes should be; they saturate common-sense assumptions and operating 'philosophies'. In effect, they constitute a situatedness which one cannot simply step out of at will – or, at least, one does so at a rhetorical rather than a practical level.

However, there is a gradual recognition of an alternative situatedness which is more than rhetorical. The most obvious indicator is the 'discovery' of personal knowledge and experiential learning. Of course, these are things which many practising adult educators have always recognized. The difference now is the recognition beyond this marginalized group. The notion that personal knowledge might be 'worth while' is obviously a major challenge to the dominant knowledge paradigm. When it is allied to the further claim that this knowledge ought to be 'accredited' and can be an alternative to formal qualifications, we are potentially in the realms of a shift to an alternative set of practices rather than marginal adjustments.

At this point I would emphasize that my remarks should not be construed as meaning that alternatives will necessarily lead to an abolition of standards. This would clearly be impossible. I am saying, however, that we could be and perhaps are moving to *different* standards which are appropriate to a system of higher education which selects in rather than selects out. Although there would still be standards, these would inevitably be more flexible and less exclusive, since boundaries would be drawn more widely. Their purpose would not be to maintain exclusiveness by 'failing' most but to 'identify the strengths and resources of all individuals and build on them' (McNair 1985: 5).

It is clear that APEL is ostensibly congruent with this purpose. On the other hand it seems to be falling into a contradiction because it also supports the preservation of existing academic standards. For example, prior experiential learning, it is claimed, can only be an alternative qualification through 'an assessment which is no less reliable and valid than the procedures customarily used to assess classroom-based learning' (Evans 1987: 17).

The assessment is entirely a matter for academic staff who may employ any appropriate procedure 'to ensure the maintenance of academic standards' (Evans 1988: 7). Furthermore, it is claimed that the APEL procedures have been tested and validated through integration with institutional procedures: 'in no sense can an accusing finger be pointed at evidence threatening the overriding responsibility of the CNAA and its associated institutions for maintaining academic standards' (ibid., 17).

Associated developments such as credit accumulation are clearly seen as an alternative way for potential students to attain *existing* standards, and indeed they take those very standards for granted.[4]

However, the most obvious point relates to the earlier discussion of the 'ownership' of experiential learning and the rigorous procedures by which the latter is to be assessed and 'accredited'. 'Objective' assessment and personal ownership are incompatible since the criteria for assessment are those implied by traditional academic standards. At the same time the 'rigour' needed to ensure that traditional standards are reached makes the whole procedure mechanistic, time-consuming and potentially demoralizing – dangers echoed in this plea that APEL 'must not be allowed to become so complicated and time-consuming as to present a barrier to anxious students and hard-pressed staff' (Griffin 1987: 9).

All this has led to a questioning of whether the APEL route is in danger of erecting more hurdles than the traditional route, with those following it ending up doubly disadvantaged. The alternative route might be taken only by those who would equally have succeeded through the traditional route; thus large-scale widening of access would be inhibited. The system would still be selecting out rather than selecting in.

Problems in relating experiential learning to curricular change

If the learning derived from experience is to be part of a broader avenue of access to higher education, it would seem to follow that this must have some effect on curricula: 'ultimately the assessment of prior experiential learning cannot be tacked onto existing programmes of study which fail to recognize the value of prior experience, the importance of a student-led curriculum' (ibid., 6).

Perhaps the most obvious example of change within higher education is the move towards modularization of courses. By giving greater flexibility and scope for negotiation modular schemes can be more student-centred. Although there is no general causal relationship between the development of APEL and the growth of modularization the important thing is that modularization and associated credit schemes can facilitate the use of experiential learning.

The structure and organization of courses is a consequence of the dominant paradigm of higher education and its knowledge tradition discussed earlier. In a sense, modularization can be accommodated within this tradition and a greater degree of student choice need not be incompatible with it. On the other hand, as we have seen, there is a tendency in APEL which, whilst supporting modularization, seems to be advocating the more radical position of replacing the dominant knowledge tradition.

The discussion so far would suggest that APEL is ambivalent on this point. Whilst appearing not to do so it actually fits in with the existing paradigm, although potentially it could be seen as more congruent with the emerging paradigm. Let me briefly explain this.

First, the APEL process seeks its justification and its very discourse within the terms of the existing paradigm. At root, it is based on the assumption that conventional formal qualifications are the norm and anything different has to prove it is as good. Second, APEL seeks to construct a means whereby its alternative admissions procedures can be seen to be as consistent as A levels, thus justifying a new approach which still preserves existing standards. Third, there has been a gradual move within APEL from the assessment of learning to the assessment of competence with an accompanying emphasis on quantification and the demonstration of predefined behavioural objectives. The consequence is that competence-based admissions criteria replace process-based criteria. Fourth, the desire for institutional acceptability is leading to procedures which are formalistic and technicist to the extent that they are becoming barriers in their own right.

What needs to be recognized is that, in the final analysis, the problem of access is not really about one set of procedures as against another but about attitudes and orientations. APEL tries to address itself to these but ultimately fails because it has allowed itself to become ensnared in procedures. In this regard it is interesting to note how the US experience, where APEL is now firmly established, is often quoted favourably as an exemplar of what could happen in this country. This however neglects the fact that in the USA higher education operates within a different paradigm. Education is seen as a right for all rather than a privilege for some. It is considered a means of self-empowerment where people are expected to determine and be in control of their own learning needs. So the APEL procedures in the USA, whatever their difficulties, at least operate within a congruent paradigm and thus within a framework of positive attitudes, orientations and policies.

Furthermore, without these, the relationship between experiential learning and the claim for responsive curricular changes remains problematic. After all, what would be the point of curricula based on prior learning if the overall paradigm remained unchanged? As Percy (1985) points out, it would simply lead to a perception of such curricula as 'second-rate' with adult students fearing for the credibility of their degrees.

Conclusions

It may well be that, if a significant increase in the number of adult students in higher education requires a change in attitudes, then the only way to bring this about is to have a broad rule for entry along Swedish lines. The usual arguments against this, outlined earlier, revolve around the fears first, of high drop-out rates and second, of diluting academic standards.

On the first point, we may need to accept that a higher drop-out rate than we are accustomed to is the price to be paid for a more open and flexible system. The fear of a higher drop-out rate is a consequence of an obsession with difference, boundaries and exclusions which, as we have seen, is the root of the problem.

Of course, this does not mean that we can ignore the question of whether adult students could cope. Rather, our concern should be redirected to how they can best be *helped* to cope. Here, a whole battery of enabling means are available from access courses to student support and counselling services to more recent innovations such as the Student Potential Programme,[5] all of which could be further developed. It is within this context that APEL should be properly located.

In essence, further development needs to be based on the original and profound insight of the experiential learning movement that getting more adult students into higher education is about empowerment and thus the starting point and emphasis has to be persons rather than techniques, personal development rather than externally demanded rigour, potential rather than prior learning, and confidence rather than competence. Although APEL in some respects does still have this emphasis (Storan 1988), there is also a sense in which the basics have been forgotten.

APEL, even as it has currently developed, undoubtedly is and will be useful. For some, the procedures may be entirely appropriate for what they wish to do, and there are areas of study definable through behavioural competences where the APEL procedures fit well. Furthermore, a sounder case could be made that the procedures are more appropriate where potential students wish to claim advanced standing. This is likely to become relevant and attractive with the increase in modularization and credit schemes and the likelihood of self-funded studies. However, the current problem with APEL is that as a supposed panacea it can easily become a restrictive and suffocating strait-jacket rather than one amongst many means of helping to broaden access. If we are to make further progress we have to accept a general commitment to the idea that potential adult students have experience and expertise which can be a resource for learning in higher education. However, accepting the further commitment that this experience can *only* be used in the APEL way is something else again.

The fear of diluting academic standards is bound up with the dominant knowledge-centred paradigm. Traditionally, the task is seen as one of inducting students into a certain kind of élitist academic culture. As a consequence, the institutions of higher education have, on the whole, never felt the need to adapt themselves to students. On the contrary, the assumption has been that students adapted to them on a 'take it or leave it' basis.

With a different paradigm which is more student-centred, institutions would have to provide a greater variety of flexible learning opportunities linked to a widening of access and changes in the structure and organization of curricula. Here, induction into an élitist academic culture would no longer be appropriate. The needs and circumstances of students rather than institutional requirements and traditions would be the first priority. Of course, this in itself would be an academic culture but it would be less restrictive and would inevitably mean a reappraisal of what is now acceptable as an appropriate standard.

Any reappraisal would inevitably have implications for what it means to be qualified for higher education. Student-centred institutions where adults constitute a significant proportion of students could not function without a flexible interpretation of qualification for entry.

Being qualified means being capable or suitable. Higher education currently interprets the former as the ability to surmount barriers which inevitably only a few can surmount and the latter as the disposition to absorb prepackaged knowledge and élite culture. Such a conception, however, is neither inevitable nor necessary. As we have seen, capacity and suitability can be conceived in holistic terms where the emphasis is on the process of, and the potential for, learning.

Notes

1 'What is so important about continuing education and training?' *Skills Bulletin*, 6, 1988, Sheffield, Training Commission.

2 In a recent speech, the Minister responsible for Higher Education clearly stressed the functional value of widening access to higher education. See 'Widening access to higher education' – conference report, 25 April 1988, AUT/SCUE, 12–23.
3 An example of the power of standards was the government's rejection of the Higginson Report (*Advancing A Levels*, 1988, London, HMSO). Press comment unanimously took the view that the government's precipitate action was due to the fear that the broader A-level study recommended would lead to a lowering of standards.
4 This position was, for example, strongly endorsed by CNAA speakers at the regional seminar on the Credit Accumulation and Transfer Scheme, 28 October 1988, Oxford.
5 The Student Potential Program (SPP), extensively used in the USA, is another means of facilitating non-traditional entry. Unlike APEL, however, it does not seek to assess prior learning but to gauge potential through constructing a profile of capabilities and motivation.

References

Bainbridge, P. (1988) *Taking the Experience Route*, London, Council for the Education and Training of Youth and Community Workers.
Buckle, J. (1988) *A Learner's Introduction to Building on Your Experience*, London, Learning from Experience Trust.
Dahlgren, L. O. and Marton, F. (1978) 'Students' conceptions of subject matter: an aspect of learning and teaching in higher education', *Studies in Higher Education*, 3, 25–35.
Evans, N. (1983) *Curriculum Opportunity*, London, FEU/Longman.
Evans, N. (1987) *Assessing Experiential Learning*, London, FEU/Longman.
Evans, N. (1988) *The Assessment of Prior Experiential Learning*, London, CNAA.
Gorringe, R. (1987) *Handbook for the Assessment of Experiential Learning*, London, Learning from Experience Trust.
Griffin, C. (1987) *Assessing Prior Learning: Progress and Practices*, London, Learning from Experience Trust.
Kemmis, S. (1985) 'Action research and the politics of reflection', in Boud, D., Keogh, R. and Walker, D. (eds) *Reflection: Turning Experience into Learning*, London, Kogan Page.
Kim, L. (1982) *Widening Admission to Higher Education in Sweden*, Stockholm, UHA.
McNair, S. (1985) *The Student Potential Program – A Report*, Leicester, UDACE, unpublished.
Percy, K. (1985) 'Adult learners in higher education', in Titmus, C. (ed.) *Widening the Field*, Guildford, SRHE and NFER/Nelson.
Perry, W. B. (1968) *Forms of Intellectual and Ethical Development in the College Years: A Scheme*, New York, Holt, Rinehart and Winston.
Rybash, J. M., Hoyer, W. J. and Roodin, P. A. (1986) *Adult Cognition and Ageing*, Oxford, Pergamon.
Saljo, R. (1987) 'The educational construction of learning', in Richardson, J. T. E., Eysenck, M. W. and Piper, D. W. (eds) *Student Learning*, Milton Keynes, SRHE/Open University Press.

Simosko, S. (1988) *Assessing Learning*, Columbia (Md), Council for Adult and Experiential Learning.

Sinnott, J. D. (1984) 'Post-formal reasoning: the relativistic stage', in Commons, M. L., Richards, F. A. and Armon, C. (eds) *Beyond Formal Operations: Late Adolescent and Adult Cognitive Development*, New York, Praeger.

Storan, J. (1988) *Making Experience Count*, London, Learning from Experience Trust.

Usher, R. S. (1986) 'Reflection and prior work experience: some problematic issues in relation to adult students in university studies', *Studies in Higher Education*, 11, 245–56.

Part 2

Impact and Process

6

The Ideology of Higher Education

Malcolm Tight

Introduction

This chapter presents an analysis of the ideology which, it is argued, currently dominates British higher education, and goes on to suggest that much more attention should be given to a range of alternative ideologies. The chapter begins with a brief discussion of what higher education is for, and the evidence available on what its clients seek from it is then considered in this context. The nature of what higher education providers, for their part, offer their clients is reviewed, and the dominant model of provision and practice is described. The final section of the chapter explores some of the alternatives to this dominant model which might be developed further in the future.

Theory: what is higher education for?

It is something of a paradox that, while there has been a great deal of debate about higher education in the United Kingdom in recent years, there has been little serious consideration of what it is and what it is for. This is not to say that no attention has been paid to these fundamental questions, but that most of it has been superficial. Official statements are not a great deal of help here either. The oft-quoted report of the Robbins Committee, for example, deals with the aims of higher education in eight crisp paragraphs:

> what purposes, what general social ends should be served by higher education? . . . no simple formula, no answer in terms of any single end, will suffice. . . . To do justice to the complexity of things, it is necessary to acknowledge a plurality of aims. In our submission there are at least four objectives essential to any properly balanced system. We begin with instruction in skills suitable to play a part in the general

division of labour . . . secondly, while emphasizing that there is no
betrayal of values when institutions of higher education teach what will
be of some practical use, we must postulate that what is taught should
be taught in such a way as to promote the general powers of the
mind. . . . Thirdly, we must name the advancement of learning. . . .
Finally, there is a function that is more difficult to describe concisely,
but that is none the less fundamental: the transmission of a common
culture and common standards of citizenship.

(Committee on Higher Education 1963: 6–7)

The more recent Green Paper on Higher Education makes no explicit
mention of aims or purposes, though the White Paper which followed did,
in response to criticism, address the subject in two paragraphs (Department
of Education and Science 1985a, 1987). Neither the University Grants
Committee nor the National Advisory Body had much to say about the
fundamentals in their submissions prior to the Green Paper either
(National Advisory Body 1984; University Grants Committee 1984). All of
these statements merely gave the Robbins Report a general endorsement,
adding here a mention of continuing education and there, in the case of the
government, a greater emphasis on the needs of the economy and the
underlying financial constraints.

Even if we assume, as these reports appear to, that we share a reasonably
common understanding of what higher education is, it seems clear that any
discussion of its purposes has to be prefaced by caveats. Two of these
appear to be of particular importance. First, as Robbins implies, higher
education is not a homogeneous activity. In the British context, it is often
useful to distinguish between the universities and higher education as a
whole, the latter including the polytechnics and colleges (or public) sector
and private institutions as well. Until comparatively recently, of course,
higher education was seen as being essentially synonymous with the
universities; and this perception, as I will argue later on, still exerts a strong
influence on provision and practice. Second, as this illustrates, our
discussion is necessarily restricted by our particular social and historical
context. In other societies and at other times (Bell 1973; Dore 1976), we
would probably have a very different perception of the issues involved.

Broadly speaking, five main purposes for higher education have been
identified which are relevant to those concerned in the United Kingdom
today (see also Bowen *et al.* 1978; Barnett 1985; Tight 1987). I shall refer to
these alliteratively as skills development, selection, socialization, scholarship and service. These purposes are interrelated and there are question
marks associated with each of them.

Skills development

Higher education may aim to develop skills in its participants which are of
value to them, to their actual or potential employers, and to society as a

whole. The term 'skills' is being used here in a wide sense, covering the first two of the objectives identified by Robbins and encompassing both the vocational and the liberal, the general and the specific, the personal/ transferable and the subject based. It would be possible, for example, following the mechanistic logic of some of those associated with the current 'Enterprise in Higher Education' initiative (Manpower Services Commission 1987), to define all of the skills which were of interest to a particular party and to specify precisely how and when they were to be developed through higher education. Whether this strategy is followed or not, however, it may be that many such skills could be developed better, more appropriately and at less expense outside higher education. In many professional and vocational areas, of course, this is the present pattern.

Selection

In practice, this is arguably a more important function of higher education, especially in the British system where supply is closely rationed. A great deal has been written on the uses of education for selection and socialization by sociologists, though their attention has been mainly focused at the school level (e.g. Hussain 1976; Bourdieu and Passeron 1977, 1979). Higher education, following the selection function, seeks to identify and accredit individuals with higher-level abilities of certain kinds. These assessments are then used by employers and others to 'place' the individuals who have benefited from the process. Yet the certification which higher education gives to its participants is, to a considerable extent, a continuing reflection of their earlier education and social background and is reinforced by the hierarchy which operates within the higher-education system itself (Halsey, Heath and Ridge 1980). The direct contribution of higher education to the selection process may, therefore, not be that great. After all, in Britain getting into higher education is rather more difficult than coming out of it with a reasonable qualification once you have got in.

Socialization

The third purpose identified suggests such a bias more explicitly. Higher education is seen here as responsible for socializing its participants for their future roles, reinforcing and forming their values and behaviour to fit them for their intended professional and personal niches. This function is, I suspect, similar to what Robbins meant when it spoke of common culture and standards; though, to be rather more honest, you might as well call it élite culture and standards. This is close to the original experiential purpose of higher education in this country, and has always been an important part of its function.

Scholarship

Scholarship, or the advancement of learning, is also a long standing function of higher education, though its extension into research is of more recent origin. Newman, for example – though he was by then out of step with the views of his time – believed that research was best carried on outside the university which existed for the purpose of producing well rounded gentlemen and intellectuals (Newman 1852). Interestingly, this view is now emerging again in a different form with the current proposals for removing research funding from certain departments or institutions, and concentrating it in 'centres of excellence'.

Service

This function is more commonly asserted outside the United Kingdom: for example, in the United States (e.g. Trow 1969), the Soviet Union and in many Third World countries. In such systems, higher education is seen as having a responsibility to serve local industry and the community through consultancy, applied research and even advocacy. The institution of higher education is viewed as being part of the wider society rather than in some way separate from it. This attitude is now becoming more prevalent in Britain, at least at the profit-making end of the spectrum.

Somewhat cynically, a sixth purpose, shared by most institutions and systems, might be added at this point. This function could be seen as either additional or all-encompassing: namely, self-perpetuation. It might then be argued that, whereas none of the purposes outlined above are a necessary part of any particular higher-education institution's operation, self-perpetuation almost invariably is.

Expectations: what do we want from higher education?

So far I have adopted a 'top-down' approach in discussing what policy-makers and practitioners believe higher education is meant for. Using the five functions identified as reference points, I will now switch to a 'bottom-up' stance, and consider what the clients of higher education seek from it. These clients – and I mean this term to include all existing and potential users of higher education's processes and products, not just students – naturally have varied wants, and in some cases these may be inappropriate or poorly expressed. When attempts are made to translate such demands into needs which higher education is in a position to satisfy, there will inevitably be problems in reconciling their variety, so that a specific client's wants may be submerged in or compromised by those of a wider group.

Unfortunately relatively little investigation has been undertaken in this area, though there have been a few interesting research studies completed in recent years. The 'Expectations of Higher Education' project based at Brunel University has, for example, produced useful evidence regarding employers' attitudes towards first degree study. In Britain, widespread graduate recruitment is a comparatively recent phenomenon (Silver and Silver 1981), so it is perhaps not surprising that employers do not exhibit a standard view on the value of degrees:

> for many employers the value of a degree is not something which can be assessed solely in terms of the degree itself, but derives from a comparison with other available forms of experience and training. . . . The most straightforward form of evaluation lies in assessing the specific attributes which are gained during degree work, which non-graduates lack. Examples given are the ability to learn, relative maturity, the level of training. However, there is no consensus among employers about this; some argue that such qualities might as easily be developed by non-graduates and indeed some argue that it is preferable for people to undertake forms of training other than degree work, even though they still recruit graduates. . . . Three factors contribute to the value added by a degree. The majority perceive it as adding some value beyond A levels, though some do not think it is very great. Mostly, this value derives from a mix of academic and non-academic qualities which graduates are believed to acquire. Secondly, a minority put a very high value on the substantive content of the degree. A third perception cross-cuts these. Whereas the first two see values as attributes to the individual graduate, the third sees a value in the degree as a useful (if not wholly accurate) screening device.
>
> (Roizen and Jepson 1985: 63–4)

On this evidence, employers' concerns seem to be with the skills development, selection and, to some extent, socialization functions of higher education. The emphasis appears to be placed firmly on the product and its background rather than on the process and content (or scholarship) of degree courses. This may not be so true for other kinds or levels of higher-education provision. Day-release and sandwich courses, for example, which are more commonly found at sub-degree than degree level, draw employers into a closer relationship with both the student and the higher-education institution during the course. Employers may be involved in course planning, teaching and evaluation. Yet the general support which many employers give to the principle of sandwich education does not necessarily mean that they will select sandwich students for jobs in preference to those with more 'conventional' qualifications (Department of Education and Science 1985b).

Collaboration between employers and higher education also tends to be closer at postgraduate level, notably in applied research and in the provision of short, post-experience updating courses. Both parties are now being urged into closer partnership in these areas by the government, stressing the service function of higher education, despite some lingering doubts on both sides. At this level, however, the product involved is rather different, and the students (employees) concerned usually study part time and remain on their employer's payroll and under their direction.

What, then, does the student want from higher education? On the basis of a national survey carried out at the beginning of the 1960s, Marris concluded that students showed a general lack of consideration regarding their reasons for entering higher education, and for choosing to study a particular subject and to attend one institution rather than another (Marris 1964). The situation is not so different now (Higgins and Keen 1988), though it may be that student attitudes changed during the late 1960s and the early 1970s. Entering full-time higher education is seen as a natural step to take for late adolescents who come out of school with the requisite entry qualifications and social background. What higher education does to you – except in the most general terms of increasing your chances of entering desirable employment and enjoying a comfortable lifestyle (the selection and socialization functions) – is possibly too imponderable a question to address at that age.

A somewhat different perspective is provided by a recent survey of students on part-time degree courses accredited by the Council for National Academic Awards (CNAA) (Bourner *et al.* 1988). Part-time degree students tend to be older and more experienced than their full-time counterparts. Their stated aims on enrolment appear to be mainly instrumental, focusing on the selection and skills development functions apparently favoured by employers. Three-quarters gave the improvement of their career prospects as a very important reason for taking the course. Professional accreditation, personal development, further study and subject interest were also mentioned as important reasons, but these tended to be of subsidiary importance. As part-time degrees *are* qualifications, this orientation is understandable. Mature students who are primarily interested in personal development or in studying a particular subject (scholarship) may opt for less formal kinds of further or adult education, where these are available (Woodley *et al.* 1987).

Practice: what does higher education offer?

Given the paucity of information on the expectations of higher education's clients, and the generality and inconsistency of these expectations when they are known, it is not surprising that higher education remains to a considerable extent supplier-led. Those who work in higher education, particularly at a senior level, largely determine the nature of what it is that they offer to the rest of society. There is an underlying uniformity in their assumptions and practices which, despite the apparent diversity within the system (Burgess 1977; Halsey 1979), sustains a dominant model of teaching and learning.

This dominant model is strongest in the universities, and its strength there is in no small part due to the relative priority accorded to teaching as compared to other activities, notably research. It is also influential in polytechnics and colleges, most of whose staff are university trained. This influence may be increasing as a consequence of academic drift, but it is curtailed by the continued existence of alternative traditions and the greater attention paid to new developments. Although more than half British higher education – in terms of the numbers of students enrolled – is now in the public sector, the dominant university model still holds sway because the universities continue to condition the perceptions of the outside world, and much of academe, regarding the nature of higher education.

The dominant model can best be described by reference to the various characteristics of higher-education courses – entry requirements, course length, course location, mode of study, teaching and learning methods, curriculum, timetabling, accreditation, costs and control. Indeed, the model is based on the notion of the course as the ideal form of teaching provision. It is interesting, therefore, that no comprehensive analysis of course characteristics, and the reasons for them, appears to have been attempted since the time of the Robbins Report (Committee on Higher Education 1963, Appendix 2B; University Grants Committee 1964); though the Leverhulme Programme of Study did produce some interesting work in this area in the early 1980s (Williams and Blackstone 1983).

The following characteristics of the dominant model of British higher education may be identified:

- an insistence on standard forms of knowledge and certification on entry;
- entry immediately after school;
- a period of study lasting for three or four years full time, but with long vacations and a considerable amount of spare time during term;
- study away from the (parental) home, preferably taking up residence within the institution, and relatively isolated from the surrounding community;
- study leading to a degree, preferably a specialized honours degree;
- study based on and within 'disciplines', which may have little relevance to the student's prior or subsequent experience;
- the use of expert/novice forms of teaching, exemplified by the lecture and the three-hour unseen written examination, and sustained by the notion of a body of knowledge which has to be mastered;
- the majority of the costs incurred borne by the state and the student's parents.

This brief characterization is, of course, both standardized and simplified. There are many examples of provision which vary from this model in some way. This is true even within the university sector. For example, my own institution, Birkbeck College, has long concentrated its efforts on the provision of part-time courses for mature employed students during the evening. Multi-disciplinary and modular courses have become quite common in universities, though there are indications of a reversion to more traditional patterns in recent years (Hajnal 1972; Squires 1987). On some courses, students have been allowed to exert greater influence over their curricula through project work and dissertations. Sandwich courses, linking periods of study with work placements, are offered by several universities, though they remain essentially confined to institutions which had developed them before they were designated as universities. In Scotland students typically enter university a year earlier and tend to follow a more general curriculum; although there has been a shift here towards a more specialized pattern of provision.

On the fringes of the university sector greater variations from the dominant model may be found. The Open University offers mass access to modular courses, does not have entrance requirements and teaches its students throughout the country using distance-education techniques. And the University of Buckingham, to take another obvious example, is a private institution, receives little funding from government and offers a limited range of courses by more intensive study patterns.

Once we move away from the universities and into the public sector, many more examples which differ from the norm that I have described can be identified. At first-degree level, the CNAA has overseen the introduction of hundreds of new courses during the last twenty years. This has involved the wider adoption of interdisciplinary and team teaching, modular provision, professional accreditation, alternative entry and exit levels, and other 'innovations' in place of the more restrictive university-degree model (Lane 1975). Public-sector higher education is, of course, much less dominated by degree provision than the university sector. Sub-degree provision remains the mainstay of provision in most of the colleges which offer higher-education opportunities. Here a range of block-release, day-release, evening, distance and open-learning courses are frequently offered in addition to full-time courses, and the orientation is predominantly local and vocational.

The examples I have given highlight a key point in my argument. Namely, in so far as provision and practice do vary from the dominant model, then these variations are perceived by those concerned as *deviations* from that model. Each deviation has to be carefully justified and is then effectively limited and controlled, through the range of checks and balances – peer review, external examiners, validation, etc. – which exist to maintain standards within the system. As in society at large, so it is within higher education: deviations are permitted or tolerated providing that they do not go too far. Change is OK so long as it is small scale and gradual. In the great majority of cases, deviations remain confined to particular aspects of provision or to certain courses only.

From this point of view, the significant point about the Open University is not its practice of open access or its use of distance teaching but its retention of the honours-degree pattern and the three-hour unseen written examination (Perry 1976). In most institutions, multi-disciplinary and modular courses are heavily constrained by prerequisite requirements and timetabling clashes, and they normally retain conventional teaching and examination procedures. Part-time forms of provision are planned and judged in terms of their equivalence to standard full-time courses. Major deviations, such as the independent studies scheme offered by the North East London Polytechnic (see Stephenson 1980), remain very much the exception. Most practitioners within higher education are not even aware of such exceptions, and, if they are, usually do not understand them and remain highly suspicious.

To summarize, then, the dominant model of teaching which I have described retains an extensive influence and control over the provision and practice of higher education in the United Kingdom. This model may well be suited to meeting the needs of particular sorts of clients in particular kinds of circumstances. It may, for example, be an excellent means for reproducing the next generation of teachers and scholars to carry on the process (the self-perpetuation function). But it can hardly be thought of as an adequate response to all possible clients in all possible circumstances. Indeed, its unsuitability for non-standard entrants is being demonstrated now as more and more institutions try to increase their participation to compensate for the fall-off in the size of the conventional entry cohort.

Change: towards new ideologies?

What, then, are the alternatives to the ideology which I have just described? How might such alternatives be introduced, and what would be the effects of doing so? Some indication of the possibilities has already been given, in passing, in the discussion of the variations from the norm that are to be found within our present higher-education system. Considerable scope exists for the adoption and adaptation of these examples by other institutions of higher education. A more extensive appreciation of the possibilities can be had by referring back to the characteristics of the dominant model, turning these around and expanding upon them. On this basis, an alternative ideology of higher education would encompass most or all of the following characteristics:

● Entry would not be dependent upon prior knowledge or certification, or based on the achievement of some arbitrary standard, but would be open to all those wanting or needing what higher education could provide.

● Entry immediately after school would be atypical, though it would still occur, often after a short break from study. People would instead make use of the opportunities and services offered by higher education at different times during their adult lives.

- Study would not normally be thought of in terms of some finite period and would not usually be a full-time activity. Instead, it would comprise one complementary part of adult life, pursued alongside employment, community involvement and social, family and leisure activities. Higher education could then be applied to the needs and interests generated by these activities, which would themselves provide a rich base of experience to contribute to the learning process.

- Participation in higher education would not normally involve moving away from home, though this would be possible, if appropriate. Nor would it cause a wholesale disruption in the individual's existing activity patterns. Students would instead tend to make much more use of local provision, whether provided by face-to-face or distance means, or by a mixture of the two.

- Study would not usually be undertaken with a particular end qualification in mind, though a range of qualifications would be available to accredit different levels and breadths of study where needed or desired. These would allow for credit accumulation and transfer within and between different schemes of provision. Programmes of study might be specialized or more general, long-term or short-term, but designed with the individual student's needs as the first priority.

- Study would tend to be based more on real problems and interests rather than on disciplines or subjects, and would normally be related (and applied) to the student's prior and subsequent experience.

- The role of the teacher would become much more that of the facilitator: someone who would help clients to assess what use they could make of the various learning resources available to them, how best to go about it, and how to evaluate the results of the exercise. In such a system, students might be working largely on their own, in one-to-one relationships with particular teachers, or as part of groups of differing sizes, involving other students and teachers as well as associates from work or the local community.

- Clients would usually assess the results of their studies, and consider the implications for future work, together with their teachers. A range of assessment methods would be employed in addition to formal examinations.

- A significant proportion of the costs of engaging in study would be borne by the students themselves, their employers and other organizations which stood to benefit from the study concerned. The state would continue to support institutions offering higher-education opportunities and would also financially assist some students who were unable to obtain support from other sources. Since students would be *de facto* as well as legal adults, their parents' financial support would be much less common.

If the alternative ideologies outlined in this synopsis were adopted as the basis for a more varied and flexible system of higher education in this country, provision and practice would be substantially changed. Much more emphasis would be placed upon the service function than is currently the case, though this does not mean that the other four purposes identified in the first section of this paper – skills development, selection, socialization and scholarship – would be ignored. Service shifts the focus away from the institution towards the client, whether the client is an individual, a group or an organization. Institutions of higher education are then in the business of serving as many clients and as many needs as possible: 'If once we take seriously the idea that the education service is a *service*, and one which seeks to serve everybody, we are committed to fundamental changes' (Burgess 1977: 87).

These changes would not, of course, be unproblematic. They would create significantly different work patterns for many of those involved in higher education. They would also, if seriously implemented, necessitate a general expansion of the system alongside its internal restructuring. Much less emphasis would be placed on the traditional university than is currently the case. Indeed, the altered higher-education system envisaged would contain far fewer universities, but many more other institutions which would offer varied opportunities for engaging in higher learning (Carter 1980; Halsey 1987). The system would in some ways be more hierarchical than at present, but the hierarchy would be interconnected and open rather than divisive, élitist and closed. Higher education would become part of a more broadly conceived and potentially lifelong system of education, drawing in and affecting more people. It would no longer function as a brief post-school but school-like activity. It would be adult rather than adolescent.

Standards would not be neglected in such a system, but they would need to be approached from a different perspective. When an academic uses the term 'standards' today, what is being referred to is usually entry standards; that is, keeping potential students out (see Chapter 5). The hidden agenda here is a wish to ensure that the great majority of entrants successfully leave the system with a standard qualification after completing the standard period of study. What we ought to be mainly concerned about when we devise performance indicators, however, is the quality of the service offered and the effect it has on those making use of it.

The vision which I have sketched here is liable to be dismissed in some quarters, of course, as both hopelessly Utopian and impractical, even if it is considered to be desirable. It is worth stressing, therefore, that not only are changes already taking place in this direction (with pressures being exerted from a range of interests for more), but that there are parallels to be found both at home and abroad. In the United Kingdom, adult/continuing education, in both its liberal and vocational forms, embodies many of the alternative characteristics which I have suggested. Though this sector has long been viewed as marginal when compared with higher or secondary education (Keddie 1980), it is of growing significance. In an international context, on the other hand, the British higher-education system is in many ways atypical. More open access, more flexible curricula and more extensive participation are to be found in North America (e.g. Lynton and Elman 1987), Australasia and a number of European countries.

Assuming that the alternative ideological approach which I have outlined is attractive (at least in part) to others than myself, how might we aim to move towards it and away from the present structure? Clearly we cannot hope to change the current system overnight. The capacity of established institutions for inertia – for ignoring, absorbing and subverting strategies for change – has to be remembered and dealt with. Nor can we realistically expect that such changes can be easily imposed from the centre, although central government and its agencies will have a major role to play.

The government's role as the principal funder of higher education is particularly important here. For example, the current proposals for altering the methods by which students are funded, shifting the balance steadily away from grants and towards loans, will have significant structural consequences (Department of Education and Science 1988). They are likely to cause a gradual blurring of the present distinction between full-time and part-time study, as more 'full-time' students come to spend more of their time working in order to earn money to support themselves. If loans also become available for 'part-time' students not supported by their employers, and if institutions respond to such developments in a positive fashion, allowing students to vary their study loads, a good deal of flexibility could be introduced into the higher-education system. There is scope here to use changing patterns of study (and work) to strengthen the expanding links between institutions of higher education and employers, which have already been stimulated by the 'Enterprise in Higher Education' initiative and other government programmes. The government's policies regarding the future funding of institutions, in the light of its declared wish to see participation greatly increased, will clearly also be of critical significance.

The other key element in a realistic strategy for development is attitude change. This will involve altering the attitudes of those who work in higher education, while simultaneously enhancing the expectations of its clients. Providers need to be made more aware of the range of functions which their institutions can usefully serve. Staff-development activities, which are almost non-existent in some institutions at present, will need to be expanded to enable staff at all levels to gain the skills they will require to teach in different ways and to serve alternative clients. New kinds of staff with more varied backgrounds, experience and skills will also need to be brought in to supplement and extend the abilities of those already in post. Existing and potential clients – individuals, community groups, employers – will need to be reached through publicity and marketing exercises and persuaded of the expanded scope for collaboration with their local higher-education institutions. Some useful activities are already under way along these lines; the time seems ripe now for more developments.

Finally, why should we attempt to change the ideology of higher education in this way? Because higher education is not currently serving anything like all of its potential clients, and because it is not serving many of those that it does serve as well as it could. All the rhetoric which we regularly hear about the accelerating pace of change in technology, the economy and society, and the consequent need for better and more education, contains terrible and timely truths. We do need a better educated, more adaptable and more self-reliant people if we are to maintain, far less develop, our society's position in the world. But we cannot hope to bring more people into higher education, and bring them in more often, if we retain the dominant model of provision and practice that I have described. We will only attract more clients, and be of more use to them, if we introduce less rigid and more client-focused systems of provision much more widely.

References

Barnett, R. (1985) 'Higher education: legitimation crisis', *Studies in Higher Education*, 10 (3), 241–55.
Bell, R. (1973) 'The growth of the modern university', pp. 13–28 in Bell, R. and Youngson, A. (eds) *Present and Future in Higher Education*, London, Tavistock.
Bourdieu, P. and Passeron, J.-C. (1977) *Reproduction in Education, Society and Culture*, London, Sage.
Bourdieu, P. and Passeron, J.-C. (1979) *The Inheritors: French Students and Their Relation to Culture*, Chicago: University of Chicago Press.
Bourner, T., Hamed, M., Barnett, R. and Reynolds, A. (1988) *Students on CNAA's Part-time First Degree Courses*, London, CNAA.
Bowen, H., Clecak, P., Doud, J. and Douglass, G. (1978) *Investment in Learning: The Individual and Social Value of American Higher Education*, San Francisco, Jossey-Bass.
Burgess, T. (1977) *Education After School*, London, Gollancz.
Carter, C. (1980) 'Not enough higher education and too many universities?', pp. 29–45 in Evans, N. (ed.) *Education Beyond School*, London, Grant McIntyre.
Committee on Higher Education (1963) *Report*, Cmnd 2154, London, HMSO.
Department of Education and Science (1985a) *The Development of Higher Education into the 1990s*, Cmnd 9524, London, HMSO.
Department of Education and Science (1985b) *An Assessment of the Costs and Benefits of Sandwich Education*, London, DES.
Department of Education and Science (1987) *Higher Education: Meeting the Challenge*, Cm. 114, London, HMSO.
Department of Education and Science (1988) *Top-up Loans for Students*, Cm. 520, London, HMSO.
Dore, R. (1976) 'Human capital theory, the diversity of societies and the problem of quality in education', *Higher Education*, 5, 79–102.
Hajnal, J. (1972) *The Student Trap: A Critique of University and Sixth Form Curricula*, Harmondsworth, Penguin.
Halsey, A. (1979) 'Are the British universities capable of change?', *New Universities Quarterly*, 33 (4), 402–16.

Halsey, A. (1987) 'Who owns the curriculum of higher education?', *Journal of Educational Policy*, 2 (4), 341–5.

Halsey, A., Heath, A. and Ridge, J. (1980) *Origins and Destinations: Family, Class and Education in Modern Britain*, Oxford, Clarendon Press.

Higgins, T. and Keen, C. (1988) *Knowledge of Higher Education in the Sixth Form*, Banbury, Higher Education Information Services Trust.

Hussain, A. (1976) 'The economy and the educational system in capitalistic societies', *Economy and Society*, 5, 413–34.

Keddie, N. (1980) 'Adult education: an ideology of individualism', pp. 45–64 in Thompson, J. (ed.) *Adult Education for a Change*, London, Hutchinson.

Lane, M. (1975) *Design for Degrees: New Degree Courses under the CNAA, 1964–74*, London, Macmillan.

Lynton, E. and Elman, S. (1987) *New Priorities for the University: Meeting Society's Needs for Applied Knowledge and Competent Individuals*, San Francisco, Jossey-Bass.

Manpower Services Commission (1987) *Enterprise in Higher Education*, Sheffield, MSC.

Marris, P. (1964) *The Experience of Higher Education*, London, Routledge and Kegan Paul.

National Advisory Body (1984) *A Strategy for Higher Education in the late 1980s and Beyond*, London, NAB.

Newman, J. (1852) *The Idea of a University*, 1976 edition with introduction and notes by I. Ker, Oxford, Clarendon Press.

Perry, W. (1976) *Open University*, Milton Keynes, Open University Press.

Roizen, J. and Jepson, M. (1985) *Degrees for Jobs: Employer Expectations of Higher Education*, Guildford, SRHE and NFER–Nelson.

Silver, H. and Silver, P. (1981) *Expectations of Higher Education: Some Historical Pointers*, Uxbridge, Brunel University.

Squires, G. (1987) *The Curriculum Beyond School*, London, Hodder & Stoughton.

Stephenson, J. (1980) 'Higher education: school for independent study', pp. 132–49 in Burgess, T. and Adams, E. (eds) *Outcomes of Education*, London, Macmillan.

Tight, M. (1987) 'The value of higher education: full-time or part-time?', *Studies in Higher Education*, 12 (2), 169–85.

Trow, M. (1969) 'Elite and popular functions in American higher education', pp. 171–201 in Niblett, W. (ed.) *Higher Education: Demand and Response*, London, Tavistock.

University Grants Committee (1964) *Report of the Committee on University Teaching Methods*, London, HMSO.

University Grants Committee (1984) *A Strategy for Higher Education into the 1990s*, London, HMSO.

Williams, G. and Blackstone, T. (1983) *Response to Adversity: Higher Education in a Harsh Climate*, Guildford, Society for Research into Higher Education.

Woodley, A., Wagner, L., Slowey, M., Hamilton, M. and Fulton, O. (1987) *Choosing to Learn: Adults in Education*, Milton Keynes, Society for Research into Higher Education and Open University Press.

7
Putting Learning at the Centre of Higher Education

Peter Wright

Accessibility and the process of learning in higher education

The question of how to widen access to higher education is intimately associated with assumptions about what should be learned there, and how.

A convenient way of recognizing this connection is to begin by contrasting two approaches which can be discerned in discussions of access: each concentrating on a distinct, though related, aspect of the subject.

The first approach tends to dwell on *mechanisms* for access – on ways for making possible the entry into higher education of so-called 'non-traditional' students (for example, mature adults in general but, in particular, older women, manual workers, members of ethnic minorities and the handicapped). In doing so, this approach concerns itself first and foremost with such issues as the provision of special access courses, the encouragement of more flexible admissions policies, and the recognition of prior learning, whether or not certificated.

Although all these topics naturally have implications for the nature of the courses provided in higher education, that is not their main focus of attention: the present form of universities and colleges tends to be regarded largely as given.

The second type of approach, while also concerned with making easier the entry into higher education of potential students from 'non-traditional' backgrounds aims, above all else, at increasing the general accessibility of the higher education system as a whole: at identifying, and overcoming the multifarious factors which make it remote, or unattractive, to the majority of the English[1] population.

The rapid establishment of access courses, which has taken place in Britain over the last ten years or so, has undoubtedly been a necessary and effective step towards making English higher education more open – as has, also, the liberalization of admissions procedures. None the less, both – by their very nature – have served only as temporary, small-scale palliatives.

Paradoxically, the unquestionable success of access courses may itself stem, in part, from the extreme inaccessibility and exclusiveness of English higher education – which these courses are intended to counter. That is to say, it may be precisely because so small a proportion of the age group go into higher education, and so many gifted and energetic people are excluded from it, that those from 'non-traditional' backgrounds who succeed in eventually overcoming the many barriers to them do so well. After all, their perseverance and intellectual capabilities cast them as members of an élite, albeit one previously overlooked.

It would be highly misleading to assume that the success of this outstanding and highly self-selected group demonstrates that British higher-educational courses are already well suited to becoming part of a genuine mass higher-education system which could embrace a quarter or half of the population.

The very success of access courses in steeling their students against the unsupportive learning environment of much higher education has, it seems, masked the need for the fundamental changes in structure, curriculum and learning methods that will be required, not merely to make it approachable by students from new backgrounds, but even to fit it to meet the changing aspirations of the most academic young people who are now experiencing in their schools a substantial shift towards more active and independent styles of learning and assessment.

The conflict between the traditional subject matter of higher education and accessibility

One must expect problems to become more apparent in the future as higher education begins to attract (or, perhaps, feels itself obliged to seek out) students from more varied social backgrounds and in greater numbers. As this occurs, so it is likely to become obvious that there is a fundamental conflict between, on the one hand, greater accessibility and participation and, on the other, the present subject matter of higher education and the assumptions which go with it about how students should learn.

This conflict has three aspects which I shall consider in turn. The first concerns the curriculum in its widest sense: its content, its degree of subject specialization, its relationship to previous experience and subsequent employment – if any – and, indeed, the tacit presuppositions which it embodies concerning the character of the experience of higher education and the demarcation of the boundaries between it and the world outside.

The second concerns the relative power of various stakeholders, especially actual or potential students, to define the shape and content of higher education and to negotiate particular paths through it to match their own special needs and those of their sponsors – whether themselves, their employers, their parents or society at large.

The third element pertains to the aims, objectives and standards of higher education and the means by which these are established (or come to be taken for granted as self-evident) and their attainment measured.

Taken together, these three aspects, I shall suggest, determine the part played by the process of students' learning within a system of higher education: they affect the prominence given to it, the extent to which its aims are made explicit, the assumptions about how it takes place, and the part which it plays within the self-perceptions of academics and their notions of what distinguishes a successful academic career.

I shall conclude by suggesting some ways in which the process of learning may be given a more central position within higher education and, by doing so, might lead to greater accessibility.

The curriculum

It is frequently observed (e.g. Bourdieu 1973) that the content of an educational curriculum is intimately related to the social role of education in any particular society.

In general, the further its content and procedures are from everyday thought and experience, the more inaccessible the educational system is likely to be; and the more those accredited as educated are likely to stand out, and to be segregated socially, from those who are not.

This is not to suggest, of course, that education simply determines patterns of power or social distance – though it clearly plays a significant part. The relationship is complex and reciprocal; causal influences run in both directions. None the less, it is hard to resist the conclusion that a social group which succeeds in mobilising acceptance for its own particular definition of what the content and boundaries of higher education should be, wins for itself considerable social and political power.

Such a point has been made, for instance, by Detlef Müller (1988) when he suggests that a 'systematization' of German secondary education occurred between 1870 and 1920. This involved, he contends, the transformation of the *Gymnasium* from a relatively comprehensive form of secondary schooling into a specialized institution which concentrated on preparing its pupils for university. This change was brought about through the *Gymnasium* concentrating on a general, Latin-based curriculum which differentiated it sharply from the lower-status forms of secondary schooling which were brought into existence underneath it.

Müller argues that a major force in bringing this process about was the desire of the educated upper-middle classes to secure and improve their social position at a time when it was under threat from economic forces.

Not surprisingly, times of major social change and conflict have often, too, been occasions when the content of higher education has been bitterly contested. In England this has been true both of the Interregnum of the seventeenth century, typified by the fascinating polemics between Seth Ward and John Webster in 1653–4 (see Debus 1970; Webster 1975; Wright 1981) and of the mid-Victorian period (see Rothblatt 1968; Slee 1986).

Further evidence of the general connection between the content of the curriculum and the accessibility of a higher-education system is also suggested by international comparison.

It is surely no coincidence that England has both one of the lowest HE age-participation rates among developed countries and also a curriculum in which specialization in a single discipline is particularly dominant.

The prevalence of the single-subject degree has, in turn, reinforced specialization in study at A level because, in many subjects, higher-educational institutions have felt it necessary to insist that entrants to their courses should already possess a high level of specialist knowledge in the subject they intend to study. Thus, for example, until recently it has been all but impossible to enter an engineering degree course without A-level passes in mathematics and a physical science subject – something hard to achieve for those who have not studied A levels at school.

The changing balance between stakeholders in higher education

The nature of the curriculum is closely linked, of course, to the relative power of different groups holding stakes in the functioning of higher education. In the past, as A. H. Halsey has argued (1986), the activity of western universities has been successively dominated by the Church, the aristocracy and, finally, from some time in the late-nineteenth century, by the professors themselves – a situation which he believes is now in the course of transformation into one of democratic control, where the university will be shaped in dialogue with the needs of the various groups that constitute society as a whole.

Such a transformation has profound implications for the nature of the power of academics as a profession. Their ascendancy over higher education for roughly a century, to which Halsey draws attention, seems to be an example of what sociologists of work would describe as 'occupational control' – a strategy used by a particular occupation group (though not necessarily consciously) for shaping and controlling the circumstances of its work so as to achieve the highest possible status and rewards for its members.

The form of occupational control exercised by academics has, I suggest, been akin to what, in other contexts, Terry Johnson has defined as 'collegiate power': namely, a form of control 'in which the producer defines the needs of the consumer and how these needs should be catered for' (1974: 45).

It has not been customary, of course, to think about English higher education in terms of 'producers' and 'consumers' – pastoral and sacerdotal metaphors have probably been more prevalent; even today the imagery of the market may seem tendentious and distortative.

None the less, it is hard to deny that in the process of higher education, however conceived, there are some who give and others who receive. Whether or not it seems appropriate to portray this relationship as one of exchange, it is hard to deny either that it involves, at least, some elements of power, or that changes in the balance of power among the various parties will tend to affect their relative capacity to define the nature and aims of their collaborative enterprise – higher education.

The erosion of the collegiate power of academics can be understood as part of a far broader tide of anti-professionalism that has come, over the last decade or so, to undermine all claims to opaque self-regulation, whether in the law, medicine, architecture, public administration, schooling or technology. The temper of the times, it seems, has become one of ascendant populism in which expert knowledge has often been cast into doubt and construed as the rationalization of self-interest (Haskell 1984).

But the changes in the power and authority of professionals to control, or even appropriate, particular areas of social practice need to be understood in the context of a still wider social transition from a world in which many functions and services were dominated by small groups of wealthy, high-status clients (often supporting symbiotically small groups of wealthy, high-status producers), to another where these functions and services are compelled to respond to the requirements of a mass market.

From this perspective it seems that higher education, too, will find itself obliged to yield to this new mass market and to define what it has to offer in terms that are appropriate to it, just as book publishing or vehicle production has done in the past. Many academics will find such a prospect profoundly depressing and threatening: they will see it as one in which the academy will be subjected to vulgar and demeaning demands.

It needs to be understood, however, that exposure to a mass market is not simply a one-way process, but one which also makes it possible for the producer – in responding to markets – to shape and differentiate them and to lead public taste. Just as manufacturers of cheap motor cars or personal computers themselves brought markets into being by producing goods which were not previously available, or even easily imaginable, so they actually created and formed the demand for the products which they had to sell, and helped to constitute the criteria by which consumers judged them.

There is no reason why the same might not be possible for higher education if it could find new ways of engaging with the needs and interests of the mass of the population and showing how these might be advanced through the experiences that higher education is able to provide.

Academic outcomes and conceptions of quality

Another link between the assumptions about the nature of learning dominant within a higher educational system and its accessibility is to be found in the ways in which the outcomes of the educational experience are conceived and notions of quality are embodied in practice.

Traditionally, the aims and the objectives of courses have been framed in two ways: as mastery of a certain body of – usually disciplinary – knowledge, often specified in terms of topics to be covered; or in terms of very general ends such as the development of critical awareness, certain kinds of sensibility, or habits of scholarship. In both cases the definition of these qualities has tended to be inseparable from the tacit, internal values shared by members of the disciplinary culture concerned.

As a result it has been hard, if not impossible, for those not already initiated into such a culture to gain independent access to the criteria by which quality might be judged. In other words, non-academics, or even more narrowly, all those outside a particular discipline, have found themselves unable to evaluate the quality of courses in fields other than their own, still less to judge the work of higher education more generally.

The absence of explicit, externally accessible criteria for judging quality has meant that the outsider has had either to accept the self-evaluation of academics blindly, or to question their impartiality: there has been no common ground on which critical debate might have taken place.

Such a state of affairs may have seemed unexceptionable in a world of social deference and patrician social élites; it does not today, when many traditional forms of authority are under question. Still less will it command support when higher education directs itself to the needs of a mass clientele.

Similarly, just as judgements of academic quality have been inaccessible to outsiders, and must often have seemed foreign to potential students who had not been brought up to hold the academic world in reverence, so too have been the anticipated outcomes of degree courses and the qualities required of those entering them.

This is apparent, for instance, in the continued dominance of the unseen written examination as a mode of assessment. Although, conventionally, the aims of degree education have often been couched in terms of higher-order intellectual qualities, little attempt has been made to demonstrate that these were, in fact, measured by the examinations upon which students' results and classification were largely if not entirely, based.

A related point may be made about entry to higher education. It would be quite implausible to explain the continued predominance of two A-level passes as the normal, conventional entry requirement as resulting from evidence that they represent a minimum definition of the skills and knowledge needed for the successful completion of a degree course. If this were so, it would be hard to reconcile with the success of large numbers of students in the Open University and elsewhere who lack them, or with the substantial variations, over the years, in the number of A-level points stipulated for entry to a particular kind of course.

Rather, it seems more plausible to join Fulton (1984; see also Chapter 3 of this volume) in regarding the A-level score as a 'price' which functions to balance the forces of supply and demand.

The persistence of inexplicit criteria

For long, the dominant assumptions about academic quality, outcomes, and entry requirements in English higher education seem to have been characterized by a tendency towards inexplicitness and a reliance upon tacit, traditional conventions.

Typically, calls for more accountability or for the provision of explicit yardsticks by which outsiders might judge the quality of what the academy does have been interpreted by those working within it as interference or even as a sign of hostility towards the central purposes of academic life.

In my view, such a reaction is not simply a manifestation of the persistent occupational control which academics have exercised over higher education, but has deep roots too within English political culture. It chimes with the persistent quasi-aristocratic tendencies in English political life which favour concealment, are antipathetic to open, adversarial debate – especially between conflicting groups of experts – and have been suspicious of meritocratic competition.[2]

Thus, for instance – at least until the University Grants Committee's 1986 attempt at evaluating research – the processes by which academic quality has been maintained and achievement measured have tended to be opaque and consensual rather than open, public or contested.

British higher education, it seems, may be coming to feel that it faces a predicament which is also familiar to many other kinds of professional grouping: how can it make itself more accountable and the exercise of its judgement more open, without trivializing the issues involved or lowering its standards?

It is revealing, perhaps, that when facing this perceived problem, higher education has been prone to suppose that the power of outside forces to impinge upon it is vast, yet the power of the academy to define, defend and promote its own values is slight.

That view, it seems to me, stems from the fact that for a long time higher education – by virtue of its élite nature – enjoyed in Britain a sheltered position in relation to sources of political power and legitimacy. In those circumstances, it had no need to proclaim its mission – or even, perhaps, to be very precise about what that might be. Pessimism about the capacity of the academic world to advance its values within British society must be seen in this context; it derives in part from the sudden need to promote itself among the population in general and is coloured by feelings of betrayal at its expulsion from its once privileged relationship with the establishment.

But the loss, however painful, of a sheltered, élite position is a necessary condition if British higher education is to become a mass system drawing students in large numbers from social groups who do not share the unspoken understandings of academics, nor even feel deferential towards them. The transition to such a system seems inevitably to entail change within higher education in a number of significant respects.

Achieving accessibility

These changes, I suggest, may be summed up by the idea contained in the title of this chapter: at the very heart of the activity of higher education must be placed the processes by which students learn and a concern for what may facilitate them.

To assert this is by no means simply to indulge in high-sounding exhortation. Many academics, perhaps most, already put a great deal of effort into trying to strengthen the learning processes of their students – that is not the issue. The problem is that the institutional arrangements which obtain in higher education – mechanisms for allocating resources, methods for designing courses, requirements for training, procedures for promotion, and so on – singularly fail to give significant weight to facilitating the processes of learning. Still less do they take it as the central purpose of their activity.

Not surprisingly, and irrespective of the commitment of many academics to devising effective strategies for learning, the implicit message of the day-to-day practice of academic life is that many other concerns are more important.

The first step towards redressing this state of affairs would appear to be for each institution to undertake a self-conscious review of every aspect of its administration to ensure that all procedures are designed to give great explicit, and implicit, weight to advancing the process of learning. Similar exercises should be undertaken by the Funding Councils and the Council for National Academic Awards to ensure that their procedures too meet the same criteria.

The second step would be to encourage detailed consideration of the aims and objectives of all courses to relate these to the needs, capacities, skills and knowledge of their target students.

These tasks should be made the primary and explicit concern of the monitoring, review and validation processes which already exist. Where they do not, it is important that they be set up as soon as possible.

To pursue these tasks would also, I believe, require a number of related developments: it would involve defining the end point of a degree, or other higher-educational courses, to a far greater extent than at present, and to do so in terms of explicit, and relatively specific outcomes: which would, in turn, entail fashioning forms of assessment that could be shown to measure them. It would necessitate, too, decisions about the content and form of each course being made in terms of planned outcomes, rather than allowing them to be determined, as often occurs at present, by historical accretion, or the conventional understanding of what constitutes a discipline.

Thus, for example, rather than constructing a degree course from a traditional discipline, or pieces of such disciplines, one might begin by determining from consultation with potential clients the qualities that were required from a graduate of the course (competences, attitudes, skills, knowledge, etc.) and then work back from these to decide what processes and matters for study would be most likely to produce the desired outcomes.

Also, such a shift in approach would have important consequences for admission procedures. The particular qualities and knowledge needed by students entering the course would have to be clearly specified, which would naturally mean abandoning the common myth that all students with the same initial qualifications start from the same point; and it would require the design of mechanisms by which to measure students' strengths and weaknesses along a variety of dimensions, and to draw up patterns of support tailored to their individual needs.

It might well be that the responsiveness of courses to the needs of students and other stakeholders could be increased if the processes of course design were more often extended outside the academic institution. Closer collaboration with schools, FE colleges and others engaged in education and training would aid the transition of young people into higher education. It would also make it easier for universities, polytechnics and colleges to become aware of, and evaluate, the applicability to higher education of the many innovations in curriculum design and learning which have recently enriched the education of 16- to 19-year-olds.

There are powerful arguments too for trying to involve employers to a greater extent in both the design and assessment of courses and, indeed, the processes of learning itself. This would not simply be valuable as a means for sharpening economic relevance – which can easily be exaggerated – but, above all, as a way of cultivating a feeling of common ownership in the activities of higher education and thus, indirectly, giving them a greater sense of its value to their employees.

Lastly, attention will need to be given to the problem of how to prevent activities devoted to promoting access from becoming marginal under the pressure of 'academic drift' and the continued emphasis on research as a measure of academic excellence. At present, it is by no means clear how this is to be achieved.

One tactic might be to encourage a certain amount of 'flagship' access work in high-status institutions in order to influence values and priorities across the entire system. The obvious danger of this approach is that it would amount to no more than tokenism, carried on in isolation from the rest of the institution's work.

Another tactic would be to allow, or even stimulate, differentiation between institutions. If this were to occur – and there are already signs that it is beginning – it is probable that some establishments would specialize in teaching 'non-traditional students', while others would concentrate on 18-year-olds possessing high A-level-point scores. Differentiation might mean that any given institution would become better suited to its purpose by seeking out, and cultivating a particular niche – as seems to be the case in the USA; but it would also tend to widen differences in status. It could thus be that the new kind of students would become a central concern for certain institutions only at the cost of these institutions themselves becoming marginal and losing status.

Future prospects

Although it is very far from clear in what precise circumstances the changes that I have advocated might come about, it does seem that British higher education has reached something of a climacteric: new methods of funding and governance, demographic shifts, rapid technical change, especially in the field of information technology, the coming of the single European market in 1992, these are among the many forces which are acting to dissolve old habits and stimulate new thinking. What is more, each of these factors seems likely to push towards a wider general accessibility.

The aim of this chapter has been to argue that wider access to higher education in Britain is not to be achieved, still less sustained, merely by opening up new routes into higher education for hitherto excluded groups – however desirable it may be to do this – but can be attained only if the system as a whole is transformed in certain significant respects in order to place at its heart the process of effective learning.

Notes

1 As there are significant cultural and organizational differences between higher education in England and other parts of Britain, I restrict the main focus of my discussion to the English situation. The dominance of England has, however, tended to mean that institutions elsewhere in Britain have sometimes adopted characteristics that derive from the special circumstances of English society.

   As a reminder of the cultural difference between England and Scotland, it is worth recalling, for example, that at the time of the Act of Union of the English and Scottish parliaments in 1707, Scotland, with a far smaller population than England, had four universities (St Andrews, Glasgow, Edinburgh and Aberdeen) compared with two (Oxford and Cambridge) in England.

2 Such characterizations are, of course, hard to substantiate but an interesting supporting analysis appears in a comparative study of British and American approaches to the assessment of carcinogenic risk (Gillespie *et al.* 1979). In this the authors comment:

toxicologists have been enlisted by the British government to generate a consensus and legitimate political decisions. In contrast to the conflicts among experts that characterize many American decisions in this field, British decisions emerge from a closed decision-making process with the apparently uncontroversial and authoritative support of science (p. 325).

References

Bourdieu, P. (1973) 'Cultural reproduction and social reproduction' in Karabel, J. and Halsey, A. H. (eds) *Power, Freedom and Ideology in Education*, New York, Oxford University Press.

Debus, A. G. (1970) *Science and Education in the Seventeenth Century: The Webster–Ward Debate*, London, Macdonald.

Fulton, O. (1984) 'Access and recruitment: overview' in S. Goodlad (ed.) *Education for the Professions: Quis Custodiet?*, Papers presented to the 20th Annual Conference of the Society for Research into Higher Education, 1984, Guildford, SRHE/Nelson.

Gillespie, B., Eva, D. and Johnston, R. (1979) 'Carcinogenic risk assessment in the USA and the UK: the case of Aldrin/Dieldrin', *Social Studies of Science*, Beverly Hills/London, 9, 265–301.

Halsey, A. H. (1986) Chairman's summing-up, *Higher Education Newsletter*, 11, 68–76.

Haskell, T. L. (1984) *The Authority of Experts: Studies in History and Theory*, Bloomington, Indiana University Press.

Johnson, T. J. (1974) *Professions and Power*, London, Macmillan.

Müller, D. K. (1988) 'The process of systematization: the case of the German secondary school' in Müller, D. K., Ringer, F. and Simon, B. (eds) *The Rise of the Modern Secondary School: Structural Change and Social Reproduction 1870–1920*, Cambridge, Cambridge University Press.

Rothblatt, S. (1968) *The Revolution of the Dons: Cambridge and Society in Victorian England*, London, Faber.

Slee, P. R. H. (1986) *Learning and a Liberal Education: The Study of Modern History in the Universities of Oxford, Cambridge and Manchester 1800–1914*, Manchester, Manchester University Press.

Webster, C. (1975) *The Great Instauration: Science, Medicine and Reform 1626–1660*, London, Duckworth.

Wright, P. W. G. (1981) 'On the boundaries of knowledge in seventeenth-century England', in Mendelsohn, E and Elkhana, Y. (eds) *Sciences and Cultures*, Sociology of the Sciences V, Dordrecht, Reidel.

8

Access: Towards Education or Miseducation? Adults Imagine the Future

Susan Warner Weil

Introduction

The issue of wider access is but one of many driving forces putting the impact and process of higher education under scrutiny. The following kinds of questions are now the subject of frequent speculation and, more recently, research:

- What are students learning and why?
- In what kinds of learning processes are they engaging?
- What is the quality of their experience?
- How effectively and efficiently are resources being deployed to develop the potential of new kinds of students?
- What kinds of qualities and competences are being developed and assessed, and for what purposes?
- To what extent do flexibility, openness and choice obtain with regard to learning structures and opportunities?
- Do different kinds of students experience the education on offer as 'relevant, useful and enabling'? (Ball 1988)
- Are students being helped to 'learn how to learn', for a changing world in which social relations are more complex, professional authority and the effectiveness of traditional structures are being challenged, and knowledge and information increase at a rapid pace?

Those who are concerned with higher education are trying to forge pathways through the tangled thicket of responses that such questions will raise, depending upon whose agenda is at issue: the funding councils, employers, professional bodies, validating authorities, heads of institutions or academic subject specialists. There is a rich debate about the kind of higher-education system that might best accommodate the expectations of different kinds of stakeholders.

In this chapter, students, an increasingly influential group of stakeholders but heretofore often invisible in such debates, consider the impact, process and structures of higher education. Their reflections on issues such as quality and responsiveness derive from their experience of having returned to academic learning programmes. The voices represented in this chapter come largely from those adults who are often at issue in access debates. The literature on adults as learners in higher and continuing education tends to reflect the experience of largely white middle-class adults, often North American, who as students or educators have experienced a great deal of previous formal education (e.g. Brookfield 1986; Organization for Economic Co-operation and Development 1987; Woodley *et al*. 1987). The majority who speak in this chapter, however, are adults who have demonstrated their 'ability to benefit' from higher education (National Advisory Body 1984; University Grants Committee 1984) but who have spent most of their lives believing that such an opportunity would never be available for the 'likes of them'. In this, they may be similar to other younger adults who have spent most of their school years feeling like this, and who remain underrepresented in British higher-education institutions.

The views represented here come from a multi-site qualitative research study which I have conducted over the past five years. In this I have investigated the perspectives of adults who have returned to do some kind of higher or continuing education course (diploma, degree, post-graduate degree, continuing professional development course) after an interval of generally at least five years following the end of their initial education. In this study I was concerned to know if and how their prior learning, within and outside formal education, had a bearing on their expectations and experiences of returning to a formal learning context. Through largely individual depth interviews, supported by participant observation and group interviews and discussions, I inquired into meanings about being a learner and learning during the course of these adults' lives in different kinds of situations within and outside formal education.

Broadly, 32 different kinds of learning situations provide the basis from which these adults reflect on their experiences as learners. Overall, 48 learners participated in the study over the course of 8 research cycles, each involving a different formal learning context. Twenty-three of the total 32 who were interviewed individually, and who therefore provided in-depth learning histories, left school with few or no qualifications. Only 7 in the study had experienced higher education previously.

Thirty-seven in the study were women; 6 were Black (Asian and Afro-Caribbean). Thirty identified themselves as clearly working class, 12 as clearly middle class, with 3 unknown. Nine found it difficult to make a distinction, but of this group, 5 felt more working class than middle class.

Six women were followed up, after they completed the diploma at Hillcroft College about which they were first interviewed, and had moved on to university or polytechnic degree courses. At the end of these second interviews, they had the opportunity to reflect upon the transcript of our previous meeting, at which they had anticipated their experiences of higher education. Opportunities to test out emergent themes and interpretations were built into the study at various intervals, but 9 participants were circulated with a comprehensive summary of the final cross-case, cross-contextual data analysis, on which 6 commented in writing and 3 by telephone.

The purpose of this inquiry was to contribute to a data base that could guide the direction and process of developments in access, and the teaching and learning of adults from different social backgrounds. It was hoped that the study could also help to inform planning for the kinds of institutional change and staff-development initiatives appropriate to attracting, retaining and developing the potential of a more diversified student population.

I begin by summarizing the key issues that have emerged from the study. These have mainly been organized around the conceptual formulation of disjunction and integration in lifelong learning, and I focus on these adults' experience of disjunction and integration as it relates to their expectations and experiences of returning to formal learning contexts. I then draw upon a particular aspect of the data, in which participants imagined the future from the perspective of their past needs and experiences as learners. They spoke about the kinds of relationships, learning processes, structures and higher-education systems that, in their experience, would help to enhance quality and responsiveness in higher education, in relation to new kinds of students such as themselves; and these themes are discussed in turn. In the last section I consider some of the implications for those concerned with widening access and suggest that not only structures and processes but preconceptions need to be reassessed.

Disjunction and integration and the return to formal learning contexts: emergent themes

Disjunction and the possibility for miseducation

Disjunction refers generally to a sense of feeling at odds with oneself, as a learner learning in a particular set of circumstances. It is not the result of a cause-and-effect relationship but rather emerges out of mutually interacting influences, as well as past and present experiences of being a learner in different kinds of learning contexts (formal, nonformal, informal; see Weil 1986). A sense of disjunction can be felt to be associated with who one is, where one is, and how one's present experience as a learner relates to previous or concurrent experiences, within and outside the formal learning context. Disjunction can be associated with feelings of alienation, anger, frustration and confusion. In this study it always refers to a sense of fragmentation and involves issues of both personal and social identity.

Disjunction sets up the potential for education and for miseducation (Dewey 1938; Jarvis 1987), depending upon mitigating circumstances from the past and in the current situation. When miseducation results, thus 'arresting or distorting the growth of further experience', the overall sense of identity as a learner (incorporating notions of personal and social identity) can be fundamentally undermined. Certain kinds of social conditions can lead to the damaging effects of such an experience becoming internalized.

Alternatively, by chance, design or conscientious planning on the part of educators, disjunction can be constructively 'made sense of' and managed. This is especially true when various partners in the learning context become more responsible and accountable for what is occurring. This creates the possibility of future actions that can simultaneously compensate for, anticipate and manage disjunction.

There are, however, academic learning situations that, by design, intent, or tradition, afford little or no possibility for individual or collective structured reflection on what it means to learn in that situation or on how the situation might be made more effective. The management of disjunction under such circumstances may be more challenging for some learners. The extent to which adults feel able and willing to cope with disjunction, and the concomitant feelings of isolation and lowered self-worth that can be generated, seems to be tied up with many factors. These include the influences of previous learning and assumptions about education at home and school; experiences of learning and being a learner as an adult within and outside higher education; one's self-concept and overall sense of self-esteem at that time in one's life; the quality of the support and relationships available within and outside the educational situation; and the kinds of compensating experiences available at the time in the overall learning environment.

In this study, adults described experiences characterized by a sense of disjunction in relation to the following:

- their expectations of and their initial encounter with the formal learning context (including the level and quality of support offered).
- the degree of continuity between the new learning experience and prior ones, both within and outside formal education.
- their experience of the assumptions and approaches operating with regard to teaching and learning, and the extent to which these jarred with prior expectations and assumptions about learning, based on experience elsewhere.
- the ways in which social differences and power relations were experienced and managed in the learning environment.
- the extent to which core aspects of their personal and social identity felt threatened or at risk in that environment.
- the management of multiple and often conflicting roles (especially for women in the study).
- the impact of contradictions between tutors' private and public stances.

- the kinds of knowledge that were allowed or disallowed as a focus for critical reflection and analysis (e.g. experiential, intuitive, practical, propositional; dualistic or contextual and relativistic (Perry 1981; see also Weil, 1986)).
- the ways in which it was expected that knowledge and knowing could be legitimately explored in that learning situation (such as through logical argument, supported by evidence, or through building and creating knowledge, drawing on sources including learners' experience).
- the nature of the dialogue, relationships and learning processes experienced in the formal learning context.
- the ways in which personal development and change were occurring: in spite of or because of what was occurring in a particular learning situation.

Integration as equilibrium

On the other hand, integration within this conceptual formulation implies that one's sense of personal and social identity does not feel itself to be fundamentally at issue, or at risk, in a particular learning environment. Integration tends to be associated with a sense of equilibrium, or an 'all of a piece feeling'. Integration does not necessarily give rise to learning itself, but rather helps to create the conditions conducive to an individual learner being able and willing to learn in a particular learning situation. In other words, there is potential for benefit, and for education. Integration thus need not be associated with intensely positive feelings.

For example, adults who have moved in and out of formal learning contexts throughout the course of their lives, and who experience little discontinuity in the assumptions and expectations about learning operating across those various situations, can feel a sense of integration upon entry and in their overall experience of subsequent comparable learning environments. What they achieve in that situation is tied in with other kinds of influences within that context and within themselves (see, e.g., Entwhistle and Ramsden 1983; Marton *et al.*, 1984; Richardson *et al.*, 1987; Ramsden 1988).

Integration as heightened self-validation

Integration can also refer to heightened feelings of self-validation, arising out of a particular learning situation. In this study, this sense of integration arose out of the extent to which a new situation compensated for prior experiences of disjunction elsewhere. Alternatively, it emerged as a resolution to disjunction involving some kind of invalidation of previously held beliefs, ideas or meanings. It is within this context that disjunction can be experienced as a constructive starting point for learning. The critical difference between the experience of disjunction as an enabling rather than a disabling experience lies in the kinds of values, purposes and relationships which obtain in the learning situation. A critical factor is the nature of the support available to guide the learner through the sense of confusion and fragmentation generated by the experience of disjunction and which enable him or her to steer a path through it towards significant learning and change. (See also Mezirow 1978, 1985; Perry 1981; Taylor 1986; Jarvis 1987.) In this study, such situations tended to be characterized by the adults concerned as feeling valued for who they were as people, and for their prior experience. Learning entailed active involvement and interrelating. Conditions associated with cycles of disjunction and integration, and indeed an overall sense of integration itself in connection with academic learning programmes, included the following: the active use and appreciation of different forms of knowledge (e.g. experiential, tacit, practical, propositional), the making of connections across disciplinary boundaries, and a positive valuing and use of personal and social differences within a group. For many learners in this study, to experience learning situations characterized by such conditions and an overall sense of integration, often served to repair severely damaged confidence and self-esteem, and to compensate for prior experiences of education.

Compensating influences

Alternatively, a relationship with a particular tutor could positively mediate an overall sense of disjunction with regard to that course or learning context as a whole. Others found that experiences of disjunction on a course could be positively mediated by prior experiences (such as access courses, or 'returning to learning programmes') in which confidence had been built, and self-esteem with regard to one's learner identity and potentiality began to develop. Relationships with peers and spouses also played a vital role in enabling learners to make sense of and manage experiences of disjunction. None the less, many of the learners in this study seemed to have required repeated experiences of integration to enable them to feel sufficiently resilient and able to withstand and indeed manage forces which could otherwise damage them. Even then, the path of the development of such resilience and confidence was by no means linear. Certain situations could spiral the learner back into feeling the scars of prior experiences, although in this study no one experienced the feeling of going back to 'square one': earlier experiences that had given rise to a sense of integration had created an internal store upon which to draw when necessary. To survive, and thrive, in academic contexts, however, it seemed that some of these experiences needed to have occurred within formal education.

Imagining: experiencing learning as 'all of a piece'

It would be well beyond the scope of a single chapter to illustrate the many ways in which the concepts of disjunction and integration are grounded in the data. Here, however, I shall draw upon a specific block of material from the study, which was generated in one of two ways. During the course of the initial research cycles, I would often ask participants directly about what they wanted and needed from teachers in higher and continuing education. In later cycles of the study, however, I began to use a role-play approach to get at these needs from another angle. I would ask participants to imagine that I had just finished my PhD, was an expert in a particular subject, and that my first teaching job was with adults such as themselves, many of whom had left school with no qualifications and had been away from education for some time. I suggested they advise me as to how I might best approach this challenge, basing their advice on their own experience as a learner in higher education.

Each of these approaches involved participants in a particular kind of imagining process in relation to their needs and previous expectations. In undertaking it, they teased out the kinds of learning situations and relationships that they saw as conducive to integration and thus to the possibility of education rather than miseducation. The role play approach, especially, helped to draw out issues which most mattered to these adults if they were to feel willing and able to learn in academic learning situations.

The following main themes emerged from the data elicited by these two techniques: the notion of personal stance in teaching and learning; recognizing and respecting differences; 'unlearning to not speak'; the role of relationships in mediating disjunction; and 'learning-in-relation'. Each of these is dealt with below, illustrating from a particular angle various aspects to the disjunction–integration formulation.

The notion of personal stance in teaching and learning

We often speak about teaching and learning as if they were simply a function of subject expertise, skill and method. These adults' accounts, however, illustrate the extent to which for them, the quality of teaching, and indeed of learning, is mediated by the 'personal stance' of the teacher. I use this term in the sense of Salmon (1988, 1989) who suggests that 'the *material* of learning has traditionally been viewed in different terms from those that define the learner' (1989: 231). For Salmon, the metaphor of personal stance lays emphasis on the personal positions of teachers and learners, and how they give meaning to their learning:

How we *place ourselves*, within any learning context, whether formal or informal, is fundamental. This is not just a matter of 'attitude', in so far as it defines our own engagement with the material; it represents the very stuff of learning itself . . . how we position ourselves towards [each other] in any educational setting . . . is what governs the limits and possibilities of our engagement together, what shapes and defines the material we construct out of that engagement.

(1989: 231)

In the accounts which follow, these adults' perceptions and experiences of teachers' personal stances towards them as adult learners are seen as vital to their feeling able to enter into the possibility of education.

For example, Gaynor was a working-class woman in her mid-fifties who returned to do an academic diploma which would enable her to go on to a degree course. She had worked largely inside her home for many years and had little confidence and low self-esteem when she entered Hillcroft College. Speaking within the context of the role-play described above, she implores me (the new teacher) to

remember what it is like to have no knowledge of that subject at all. I have found that here. I think it is very difficult for the tutor to put themselves in the position of the student who has no knowledge whatsoever, so I think it needs a fairly gentle introduction. . . .
SWW: *Anything as to how I introduce. How I relate to students?*
GAYNOR: I suppose attitude. Not to be patronizing. That's an obvious thing but I think they can slip into that attitude. I suppose that's the same thing as patronizing. Not to stand back as the great authority! —— is very good at it. . . . She is marvellous. I don't know quite what it is, but her manner is very good. I think also because she is very prepared to talk about her own inadequacies.
SWW: *To show a bit of herself?*
GAYNOR: Yes and it means she is more someone you can relate to.

Gaynor to some extent can identify the kinds of skills and attitudes she needs. She gropes for words but conveys the extent to which one teacher communicates a sense of who she is as a person, thus opening up possibilities for relating and learning.

Rhoda, long unemployed and with little sense of self-esteem or direction, stresses the negative impact of tutors who position themselves towards their material, rather than towards the student. She is describing here the extent to which she had felt progressively silenced by what she had experienced from certain tutors.

They have to be hearing what *they* have to say. I constantly get interruptions which makes me feel, 'Should I be here?' . . . And they are always so busy. I always feel I'm taking up his time.
SWW: *What about attitudes?*
RHODA: I always have the feeling with my tutor that he's 'in the know'.

He does most of the talking. He should be more laid back and draw me out more.

Frank was a lower working-class man and previously a labourer who read 12–15 books a week, across at least six subject areas. He re-encountered a former teacher whose previous attempts to encourage him at school had been 'too little, too late'. She persuaded him to return as a mature student to an FE college to do O levels. He did A levels there also and, after an interval, went on to a polytechnic course. He had, however, consistently encountered structural and attitudinal barriers in his attempts to engage with formal learning contexts. He felt that, during those years of struggle, it was only in political groups that he was able to find the intellectual stimulation and dialogue that he actively craved. Here, he too emphasizes the importance of a personal and social dimension in his interactions with teachers. Unlike many of the women in the above accounts and those that follow, however, he communicates a certain resilience and autonomy in his expressed wish for confrontation and challenge.

Their responsibility is to point out the central core of the basic theory, to confront you as an individual. You can then decide if you agree or not. . . . But they must draw people out. Reach for their potential. Help you to engage with central theory. It is an interactive relationship. This requires knowledge, skills and personal qualities. Also, they must be sensitive to personal problems because these will distort the learning process.
SWW: *What skills?*
FRANK: An intellectual grasp. A degree of lucidity with which they can explain. Must be evaluated on the extent to which they can facilitate people's interest in and ability to deal with knowledge and their capacity to incorporate within the learning situation the views of the students. Especially the older ones. Which may be in *direct contradiction* and which may *not* be supported with six million academic references, but practical experience.

Fran was a working-class woman who throughout her initial schooling aimed to be a hairdresser. She eventually became a lecturer and teacher in this field, to the amazement of her family, since they had always seen her sister as the 'academic one' and Fran as the 'practical one'. The ways Fran strived to use her intelligence and creativity in each work situation, however, often seemed to put her at odds with colleagues. One summer, after she had left an unsatisfactory work situation, by chance she came upon information about the local polytechnic's willingness to accept adults without A levels. She inquired, out of curiosity, and was offered a place. She describes running all the way home, in panic and disbelief. She spent the entire summer trying to persuade officials that, if they were willing to give her a grant to study for three years, they could give her one-third that money to set up her own business as a hairdresser. Failing in this, she began at the local polytechnic in the autumn.

Fran speaks about the need for someone 'with communication skills' and for tutors who can 'break into a language that you can understand.'

> If I could understand what they were saying it would be lovely. They need to talk to me and explain it to me. I would expect them to be positive and encouraging. Usually, if you ask a question, you end up with a negative. . . . They don't use a reinforcing way of learning. They just sit there and rub up their own ego. . . . One thing they need to know is how to be a teacher. That's the one thing they *don't* know.
>
> SWW: *What does that mean to you?*
>
> FRAN: If I have to sit and take notes for an hour, which is far too long, I need something that is constructed in a sane pattern. So when I read my notes afterwards, they make sense to me. . . . They ought to be able to use experience, and break into the lecture, without feeling you are taking them off at a tangent. . . . They can't convey what they know. . . . They don't connect it with anybody else's subject matter.

I believe Fran and the others highlight the divide that adults can feel between themselves and their expectations of academic learning situations. Moreover, her own experience as a hairdressing lecturer, after years of apprenticeship and training, led her to feel incredulous that teachers in higher education had preparation only in their subject area.

Recognizing and respecting differences

Adults in the study continually spoke about the importance of being acknowledged and respected for their differences. The interview questions constantly revealed ways in which a failure – in actions, not just words – to recognize and respect their differences could prove a source of disjunction.

Connie was a middle-class woman who had worked entirely inside her home and had taken primary responsibility for parenting. She reached a point where she bought an IQ book, because she felt no better than a 'cabbage'. She returned to higher education via an FE college that catered particularly for mature women returners. This experience had been characterized largely by integration, with continual discovery and challenge emerging out of the quality of the relationships with peers and tutors. She found her transition to the polytechnic unsettling in many ways. Here she emphasizes the effect of different kinds of personal stances of tutors upon her as a learner. In particular, she highlights a confusion she elaborates in other parts of our interview: namely, that tutors are adult learners too, and therefore *how* can they not understand the differences? She speaks about the need for tutors to remember that they *too* are mature students and to use that as a way of relating to mature students. They come with experience. How they see us affects how they interact. They must be helped to see that. [But they imply], 'If you're motivated, you'll get it.' Your pressures are seen as a testing ground. For example, 'You'll be a good [names occupation]' rather than *realizing* the pressures you are under. I wouldn't want the structure and the knowledge to be changed. Just to have more time, and more emphasis on motivation. But sometimes, I just cannot cope. There must be a positive discrimination towards older people.

Todd, a working-class man, had struggled all through initial schooling, feeling out of place in terms of his artistic interests. Throughout his education he had felt pressured to be someone he was not, symbolized by the efforts of teachers to turn him from left-handedness to right-handedness. He left school with no qualifications and went to work in the markets. Before returning to do a degree, he had been both unemployed and a musician, having discovered a relationship with another musician through which he could develop these interests and talents. Here he elaborates on the differences cited by Connie and, like her, stresses the pressures on him in terms of the complexity of his life: in this case, as a musician, as a parent, as one of many in this situation who were not well heeled financially, and who had anything but the prior learning and life histories of more traditional students. He asserts the need for tutors to recognize

that we're not just students. We have an outside life too. We suffer the same problems. We're not purely a brain. We're human beings. That's the way it is with normal education. It's not right. But they think they can group us in a lump. Shows a lack of responsibility. Here, they still teach you like you were secondary school. It's the same process: socialize, work, see tutor. But they *must* know about people like when they are starting to flag. Like this guy who was living in a squat and had to take casual work for four weeks. They have to have skills of working with people: diverse people. People who were delinquent, mentally ill. It's not so much they are misfits. There are lots of really clever people. It's just that they should not be treated as if they were academics. . . . No one here has asked me what I am going to do, much less what I have done.

Recognizing differences for a number in the study also meant recognizing previous damage and actively repairing confidence, particularly in the case of women. Sally is another working-class woman who experienced redundancy and separation before her return to study at Hillcroft. Initial education for her had been fraught with one trauma after another. Here she stresses differences of age and experience, as well as those of gender, in her advice to me as this 'green but expert' tutor:

[You] must take into account that they *are* adults. Any ideas you had about teaching children. These will not be terribly useful. . . . First of all, you must take into account that they have other responsibilities. For example, people here have children. Different times, sickness. Your lectures may be disturbed. Therefore, it will be less of a regimented regime. And you may have to backtrack on information rather than everybody sit up straight and carry on. You must be very patient, because most women have the impression that they are no good at things, and certainly, that they don't have as much clout in the world as men do and you have to be patient in showing them that this is not necessarily so. You're repairing confidence. I think you may have to give a lot of your time to thinking out lectures and making them relevant to people's day-to-day experiences. And to introduce subjects. If you told a woman on the street with two kids, you were going to learn Schopenhauer today, she would probably run away screaming. So you have to work out with your lectures, how to get the deep elements over to people, in a way that doesn't frighten them before they even start.

Later on, still in the role-play, Sally gives me practical advice about how to minimize disjunction (as I later interpreted this), particularly for women, during the course of group discussion. Here she speaks out of her experience of returning to formal education in a women's college where small groups were a key feature of the learning environment. She stresses the importance of recognizing differences in women's pacing and patterning in group dialogue. Once again, the relational aspect of teaching and learning emerges as a central feature:

I think that is one of the pivots of adult education. *Don't* have too big a group. They will be overawed. If so, some will be quite vocal. You must use them, take their ideas, but don't let them overawe the others. Encourage those who are quiet. You've got to encourage people to speak, those who are quiet. Don't bully or say, 'What do you think?' I would need time to think about that, but I am sure that there are subtle ways in which you can include people in small group discussion. But the women I know, the women are quite enthusiastic. But the more they get to know you, the more they will open up. I think they are also very afraid of examination situations and formal learning and they have to be very *gently* introduced to this.

Unlearning to not speak

Sally experienced considerable disjunction arising from the contrast between her experiences at Hillcroft, and her university science-based course. In the latter context, she felt an acute sense of fragmentation with regard to the treatment of the discipline, the process of learning, and the underlying assumptions about knowledge and research operating in that environment. Although there was an essential coherence across the latter three, it none the less made Sally feel fundamentally at odds with herself and that environment. The disjunction and subsequent anxiety generated by this situation focused her attention on whether and how she could cope, at the expense of academic achievement. Here she describes the other kinds of forces that can diminish or enhance resilience in a learning situation. She reinforces the findings of previous research (e.g. Aslanian and Brickell 1980) that women often return to higher or continuing education at a time of trauma or transition in their lives. Here she speaks again about the need to 'repair confidence'. Her conviction indicates how much she too had spiralled back into self-doubt in her new learning situation (see also Weil 1988):

> I have realized, being at university, young people nowadays are much more confident, but when women get to my age and are returning to learning, usually and not always, it is for a good reason. They've lost their husband through divorce or illness, and they have suffered some kind of traumatic experience and need to make a living and they are very very traumatized. In a delicate state. The only way you can describe it is that. And they need not only the ability to learn, but their confidence building. They need to be able to talk about their worries and fears and they need, perhaps, extra time given to them, because they might find it harder to learn after a big gap.

For Sally, integration entails being actively engaged in a learning process which involves actively relating to others, building on their contributions, and gently nurturing confidence. However, she and others often referred to the ways in which they could feel silenced by an intervention, often male – although few conceptualized it in gender terms, and virtually none in feminist terms. But the sense conveyed is that of feeling 'stopped in one's tracks'. Often accounts of such situations awoke memories of being negatively reinforced for being assertive and speaking with conviction. Such forces had taken their toll on women's sense of self-worth and of possibility as a learner.

Karen is a working-class woman who had worked largely in secretarial jobs, and had eventually found her way to Hillcroft. She reinforces similar themes of recognizing differences and being sensitive to feelings. She emphasizes drawing people out and building their confidence up. But she too suggests the kinds of conditions that can help people to, in Marge Piercy's words, 'unlearn to not speak'. She implies how easily tutors can, even unintentionally, abuse their power to the detriment of the learner. Later at university, Karen experienced considerable disjunction, in the form of a major writing block on a humanities course. Although the method of teaching was largely in small groups, she felt severely silenced by certain attitudes and stances on the part of some male tutors and later a male counsellor. Here, speaking from the perspective of Hillcroft, before moving into this learning situation, she talks about the need for tutors to approach people,

> on a one-to-one basis, a personal basis, not as teacher–pupil.
> SWW: *What would I need to know about people?*
> KAREN: To be able to assess personalities. To know who can take harsh criticism and the people who need drawing out more. To know the things that draw them out. Know people's names [laughter]. That sounds silly, but if you call people by their names, you get this sort of bridge. But the main thing is to treat people as an adult, rather than teacher–pupil. . . . Don't be too harsh in your criticism in certain situations. Not to be patronizing, but put yourself in their position. These women have gone through the same situations as you have. You should approach them on a equal footing, although you are 'imparting the knowledge'. You're sharing it, not dictating it.

Godfrey and Janice also consider the kinds of learning situations that promote their development and learning to fuller potential. For them, issues of personal and social identity, and the experience of differences, are central to the possibilities of education or miseducation. In their learning situation, and in the wider world, the majority group wields a great deal of power and control over opportunity for them and other Black people.

Godfrey's description contrasts to some extent with the accounts of the women above, in the sense in which he stresses his autonomy and strength in the face of adversity. None the less, he conveys how a respect for differences and a recognition of the complex social arena within which learning is taking place can be fundamentally at issue for some adult learners. As such, he elaborates themes introduced above. Here, in the context of a group interview, he and Janice talk about what they need to feel able and willing to learn. They describe what they experience when they learn with other Black people in comparison with how it feels in an academic situation, where different kinds of judgement and power are operating, especially when they are in a room full of White people.

> GODFREY: When I am challenged and criticized by anyone, I feel every part of me is learning. When cornered, for example, on a platform, giving a speech, I am all angry and aggressive when I'm at my height. If I'm in a group of people and everyone's against me, I learn most. When I must challenge myself and assimilate what I've learned. Give different interpretations to things. Why, I enjoy people not agreeing with me. Find it beneficial, useful.
> SWW: *Does it matter who the person is?*
> GODFREY: I never feel comfortable in a room full of whites. Never relaxed. Always on guard. Automatic. Immune to it. Unconscious. I speak in a particular manner. More passive in the way I present myself. Not if in a group of Black people. [Changed body posture, language, phrasing] Whaa . . . [laughed]. More relaxed. It's *me*! [Smiled.] Can

curse, do anything. Like when you're angry, revert to your past experience. To learn fully, to be total, must be amongst Black people.
JANICE: Certainly think you have to be on guard when you are with [white people]. Depends, on position, authority. Must think of that. Must infringe on you as a person, depending on the group you are in. . . .
GODFREY: I need respect in my environment for me to learn. Plus a stable psychology!
JANICE: I feel much more relaxed with a Black community group. Because there, constantly raising other people's consciousness.
GODFREY: Also, at these times, when black people challenge you with something. But if *they* [i.e. white people] challenge you, that is *your* view and this is my view. Just leave it. No drive, no push, no encouragement to continue on-going dialogue. With group of Black people, if someone says, Black people are inferior to white, you will argue, say, 'No, no, no.' But in terms of their point of view, will read about it to see where they are coming from. But if white person, will ignore it.

In this account, they engage centrally with dimensions of learning that are at the heart of disjunction and integration. They speak about 'to feel total', 'to learn fully', 'you as a person', 'It's *me*'. They convey the extent to which a certain sense of integration in their personal and social identity must be felt, in a context of constructive support and challenge. They talk about needing 'a stable psychology' in order to derive maximum benefit from a learning situation. Here they suggest the extent to which they have felt it necessary to always be 'on guard' in the learning situation.

Godfrey and Janice experienced a great deal of disjunction on their course, but this was mediated by a number of influences: their opportunities to reflect on their experiences with other Black people, both within and outside that learning situation; their relationships with some significant-other peers on their course who could help them to keep in perspective what they were experiencing; their determination to get the piece of paper and more power, whereby they could influence the situation of other Black people; and finally, the extent to which at the end of their course, tutors began to engage with them in a constructive process of reflection and showed themselves to be valuing actively the perspectives and experiences they brought to the course. Both were involved in advising on issues of process and curriculum, in order to enhance possibilities for education, rather than miseducation.

Victoria was a working-class woman whose experiences of initial education were fraught with pain and struggle, particularly in terms of her relationships with teachers who tended to keep issues of accent and class on the agenda. Her discovery of her own intelligence as a learner came first through her vicarious experiencing of her husband's return to study: she read and wrote alongside him. She still, however, did not even contemplate that such an opportunity could be for 'the likes of her'. Her awakening to her own sense of possibility came through becoming involved in the miners' strike, and later a women's group. She learned about Hillcroft and negotiated with her husband to do the two-year diploma. Thus, the special circumstances of Hillcroft persuaded her to go there, and test her new-found confidence and sense of potential as a learner.

Victoria's experience of Hillcroft was characterized by a strong sense of integration, in ways that were coherent with the experience of learning she experienced in a women's group prior to returning. These experiences compensated considerably for the extent to which her initial education was fraught with disjunction. Here she speaks about the importance of the manner in which tutors interact with students, and the need for them actively to value adults' experiences. Within this account she betrays her own sense of vulnerability in situations where what she has written is publicly judged. In this, another manifestation of 'unlearning to not speak' becomes evident:

> Don't assume that they don't know anything, but there again, this is a bit difficult. You can't assume that they know anything at all about your subject. . . . But without talking down to them and not going way above their heads so that they are saying, 'What the hell are you going on about?' But it's amazing what life experiences, especially in groups of people, the amazing things they have done and been involved in and they add so much to the discussion. But you may assume that a student thinks it's totally irrelevant. No, it's not. I mean it. . . . Your essays and they become very precious to you and, if you've made a great boob or something, you don't really want it spelled out. Even if it's only two or three of you. Not always. But it is the building up of the confidence which is the important. . . . The ones we get on best with are the ones that are open, are friendly and seem to be genuinely interested in you actually learning something about, passing their subject and having a genuine interest in what they are trying to get over to you. Some enthusiasm for their subject always helps!

Victoria later decided to go on to a university course. My attempts to follow her up coincided with her separation from her husband.

In these accounts, from those who, not just in terms of age, but also in terms of gender, class and race, have traditionally been underrepresented in higher and continuing education, the complexities and struggles in 'unlearning to not speak' become manifest. The possibilities for experiences of disjunction, rather than integration, for miseducation, not education, become clearer.

Mediating disjunction

The possibilities for disjunction can be significantly heightened when some of the sources of disjunction remain invisible to, or are actively denied by, tutors. Darcy and Ethel illustrate how relationships can play a critical role in mediating disjunction and enabling adults to juggle paradoxes and contradictions encountered in the learning environment. For example, Ethel is another working-class woman who never associated learning with school (see also Weil 1986). She, like many others in the study, found herself on a course at her local polytechnic more as the result of chance rather than design. She experienced considerable disjunction throughout her course, particularly with regard to the emphasis placed on what she regarded as 'knowledge for knowledge's sake' and the extent to which she experienced higher education as an arena where 'they are playing intellectual ping-pong with other people's ideas' rather than creating, originating. Her project work created a kind of oasis for integration, thus playing a significant role in compensating for the disjunction she was experiencing overall: 'My only original work on this course was my research. I loved that. . . . From June to March I worked non-stop.' A particular tutor also played a key role in enabling her to manage what she was experiencing. She described him as,

> absolutely smashing because he is utterly deviant. I love deviants. And he is intelligent. He is not a good lecturer, but he is a lovely person. And I can learn from him. More listening vs. making magic and he can listen to you and he is sensitive and gentle with other people. Sometimes he forgets himself, but he knows he is clever enough to annihilate others, and he doesn't ever use that.

In this account Ethel acknowledges how personal stance overrides incompetence as a lecturer. She also, however, acknowledges the personal and institutional power that tutors have, and the extent to which this can feel enhanced by the ways in which they choose to use their intelligence. Her account suggests the potentially destructive impact of such power when, for example, the norms of a course, department or institution favour attack and competitive argument as the primary means for 'building people up' intellectually. Alternatively, as in the case of Godfrey or Janice above, such different kinds of power can also combine with social power, something that was at issue for many on the course – particularly when they were confronted with learning situations where there were few people with whom they could socially identify, amongst their peers or the staff.

The kinds of knowledge forms and learning processes that dominate in a particular learning situation can combine with these other forces to have a powerful effect on the extent to which that learner feels education is possible. Darcy was a working-class woman few of whose teachers recognized her potential at school, and for whom, as for many in this study any recognition had been 'too little, too late'. She left school with no qualifications but later was fortunate in discovering mentors at work who wished to encourage her intellectual growth and development. Although there were often sexual overtones to such relationships, she none the less benefited in terms of being opened up to knowledge and possibilities for learning and self-expression that she had never been able to explore. She eventually became a secretary in an FE college, where her boss encouraged her to do O and A levels. That experience of learning, largely with other mature women and tutors who specialized in working with women returners, was characterized by a heightened sense of integration, particularly in the extent to which it compensated for prior experiences at school. Her experience of her polytechnic course was a different matter. Identified as one of the more exceptional students by a principal lecturer, Darcy speaks about her experience of confronting her favourite tutor with the disjunction she had experienced during her first two years:

SWW: *You mention teaching, learning. What do you mean by these words?*
DARCY: Learning for me equals excitement, curiosity. Even with mundane things. Even those can be stimulating to learn by looking at what is *not* obvious. Even they can involve you. . . . Teaching is *not* coming to a lecture room and reeling off a list of references in some order or presenting a stripped outline, or being defensive about critical questions or pretending. So many times in the lecture room a lecturer will defend a point. But privately, say a different thing altogether. One to one, they will state their feelings and beliefs. This is dishonesty. I can't stand that. Teaching cannot be about that. There is nothing wrong about saying, 'Here is the syllabus. You must do *that* to get the qualification. But here is what you should *know*. What we must think about. The questions we must ask.' For example, there is one lecturer who is brilliant. He 'knows everything'. [She laughed.] Once I had an argument with him and I started crying, because he just couldn't see what I was saying. It is so sad. [She told him that she found the subject area and its treatment a 'load of shit'.] He was really shocked. He said, 'That's disturbing.' I said 'Either find methods which are appropriate . . . or stop altogether because these are meaningless. You keep on doing the same thing over and over again. To what end?' He stopped and said 'I've felt that for two years.' [She became very sober.] *He* felt that, but he felt he had to keep up the pretence. And I thought, 'How sad.' Brave man. [Shook her head in disbelief.] After two years. Brave man.

Darcy highlights the tension identified by Arthur (1988) who speaks about how excessive disciplinary specialization can promote the 'mastery of minutiae at the neglect of the momentous'. The juggling of such tensions can produce painful disjunctions on the part of those who have not been socialized into a culture where they are not felt to be at issue. Sadly, Darcy decided to leave her course after the second year.

Andrea was a middle-class woman who had worked entirely inside her home until her children became teenagers, and had done a return-to-learning course. Here she gained the confidence to do a one-year diploma and then move on to a degree course. It is at this point that I interviewed her. She stresses the importance of tutors being 'honest about the limitations of the system they find themselves in' and reinforces the constructive impact of a tutor's honesty on the management of a similar disjunction. She suggests that, in such situations, it is all too easy to attribute blame to student attitudes.

> We have a tutor who is useless and in the end he said 'You'll never be any good because your attitude is all wrong.'
> SWW: *To you?*
> ANDREA: To me. Because I couldn't accept that he just put facts down and you just had to accept them when your mind was fighting against accepting them. And so I would say. . . . But instead of saying, forget about that, this other fellow took over from him, straight out of the East End of London. Great fellow. He said, 'Most of this is rubbish. It is all assumptions. But they have to teach you a basis. So just accept what's going on.' And from that moment on, you could accept it.
> SWW: *He had been honest about it?*
> ANDREA: Yes, perfectly honest and he said, at the end of this year, they will tell you to forget all about what you have learnt because it is not right. So just go through it for the exams, and he would say, 'This is the best way to go about it.' And you can just accept it then.

According to these learners, to encourage this 'unlearning' and to nurture an overall sense of integration and possibility for education demand a recognition of differences, a kind of integrity in the personal stance of tutors, and a particular kind of quality of dialogue emerging from 'learning in relation'.

Learning in relation

Women's voices predominate in this study, and in their accounts there seem to be fundamental assumptions about learning that can be at odds with the kinds of assumptions about knowledge or teaching and learning that can predominate in academic learning environments. The themes of 'learning in relation' and learning as a process of making connections recur again and again. For many adults in the study, there seemed to be a vital need to make connections, with one's life, with other disciplines, with issues that personally mattered, and with experience that was both prior to and had also emerged out of that course.

For example, Fran (quoted above) talked about how, in her experience, '[teachers in higher education] don't connect [their subject matter] with anybody else's.' For Fran, subject matter is as much 'in her' and in her experience, as it is in books or in academics' heads. There is nothing in her experience that has taught her to discriminate between these forms of knowledge, or to elevate one form above another. To deny the validity of her forms was to deny the validity of her personal and social identity, and her prior experiences of learning particularly outside formal education.

Rita's story also illustrates the extent to which not learning-in-relation, not feeling able to make connections, threatened the possibility of engagement with tutors and with academic material. She was a working-class woman who experienced considerable disjunction during her early education. To exploit her considerable intelligence she put relationships with her peers and family at risk and threatened her own sense of personal and social identity in class and gender terms. She later became a single parent, left by her husband with three small children. A support group run by Social Services enabled Rita to achieve a sufficient sense of self-esteem to attend a return-to-learning course at Hillcroft. Here, for the first time in her life, she experienced a sense of integration as a learner, particularly since relationships were not threatened. In this account she describes the effect that a particular kind of interaction can have on her willingness and ability to work in a particular subject area.Here Rita is advising me in the context of the role-play:

> They are adults first and students second.
> SWW: *What does that mean?*
> RITA: In the lecture situation, all right, so the tutor stands at the front and gives the lecture and that is reasonable and they are sort of chairing the discussion. When they are not doing that, these are people, who are not your inferiors, not children and that is something I have noticed from some of the tutors. Some of them treat me as a person, whether they teach me or not, and some treat me as a student.
> SWW: *What do these different approaches trigger in you as a learner?*
> RITA: If they treat me as an adult, I tend to respond to them as a person. You know, we are talking person to person and that means I can off duty talk about the subject or other things and, if I feel they know me and care about me, I quite like working for them, but those who tend to treat me, you know, 'This is all wrong and this is how you should be doing it', I don't know if I want to do it at all.
> SWW: *So no matter how much you like the subject, there is that tension?*
> RITA: Yeah, there is still that feeling there. Yeah, it can be seen as a challenge, but I'm not going to let you put me off this subject!

Rita is speaking here from the context of our second interview, when she had moved on to do the two-year diploma at Hillcroft. I saw her both before and after she did this course, and she conveyed a tentative but definite spiralling towards greater resilience and confidence. But she still spoke about how certain situations could quickly reopen old scars, and weaken her repaired but still damaged sense of self-esteem.

Sally speaks here also from the context of her university course where, as a result of the disjunction she was experiencing she has a heightened sense of the kinds of conditions in which the probability of integration, and therefore of education, is increased:

I think that one of the first things I would say to a student is that *everything connects*. I had no idea until I came here . . . So if I were a lecturer here, I would ask others what they were teaching so I could make the connections in my mind and then put it over to the students. Because that is one of the first things that amazed me. That no subject is an island. All interconnect and interrelate. And same with the students: they all interconnect and react with each other and need to bounce ideas off each other.

The theme of interweaving – across ideas, subject boundaries and in the context of one's relationships with peers and tutors – is vivid here.

For many of the women, not to learn in relation, and in ways that enabled them to work from and build upon their existing strengths and understandings, was to put at risk a fragile sense of self-esteem. Those kinds of conditions seemed to nurture trust in one's own voice, without feeling that powerful forces would intervene either to silence that voice, tell it it was *wrong*, or revive the feeling that to speak, to write, to create and have access to knowledge in higher education was not really for 'the likes of them'.

The context for learning: imagining alternatives conducive to wider access

In the first half of this chapter adults from the study discussed their personal experiences, meanings and feelings of disjunction and integration. In this section they answer the question of what kinds of structures might be needed to provide wider access and more effective learning for adults. The exploration of these particular topics was not an explicit or systematic focus in the research. But they often arose in the course of considering meanings and experiences of being learners, anticipating the transition to another formal learning context, or coming to the end of a three- or four-year course.

Here various adults from the study imagine alternatives from the perspective not just of their experience of higher and continuing education, but also within the larger personal and social context of their lives. In so doing, I believe they lend depth and richness, and a particular kind of grounding, for many of the arguments put forward in this book and in the wider literature about the issues we need to consider if new kinds of students are to be attracted to, retained and enabled to benefit from the many resources and existing strengths already present in higher education. The following issues are considered:

assessment
learning contexts
existing and alternative structures.

Assessment

The extent to which summative assessment procedures impinge on the quality of learning and dialogue emerges as a preoccupation in a number of accounts. For example, Janet was another middle-class woman who had lost confidence after working in her home for many years, interspersed with low-status jobs. She too returned to Hillcroft and later went on to university. She suggests that,

> for adult learners you should abolish exams. And use continuous assessment. Look at your whole contribution over all your work. Rather than this [emphasis on final examinations]. . . . The system fails a lot of people who need not fail. If they are not taught to be failing, they wouldn't. It crushes the individual. It is all too rigid, too confining. You lose your creativity.

Peter grew up in a middle-class family where his parents encouraged by every means his own achievement of his academic potential, including sending him to public school. He then sought low-skilled nine-to-five jobs to facilitate his ambitious self-managed programme of studies. Here he speaks from the perspective of having eventually gone to university and also having left it. In the full interviews he spoke at length about his concern with the lack of quality and standards and the lack of pressure on young people like himself to work or think critically. Later he returned, assisted, like Darcy, Ethel and Andrea by a tutor who was honest about the contradictions he was experiencing and who helped him to manage the disjunction he was experiencing. He graduated, and later began a post-graduate course, which he left after one year in favour of self-managed study. Here he speaks about his experience of having students in his classes who were not studying for degrees, and therefore did not require consummation through examination.

> SWW: *Can I ask you something? Do you think that influences the quality of the teaching, because they know they have people there who are there just to learn?*
> PETER: Yes, it does. I think something like a third are not working towards exams and they tend to ask more questions and tend to be more involved than the others and they are a good influence. I thought it worked and, if I had time and energy in the future, I may go back to a course like that where you just learnt for the sake of it and I doubt I will, but if I was advising someone younger, I would say 'Go for a course like that.'

Sally felt the atmosphere changed in her second year at Hillcroft when there was more emphasis placed on future examinations and destinations. She describes this here within the context of her own sense of risk taking and vulnerability at university.

I still feel at university very frustrated and I didn't think I was going to but I do and it was . . .

SWW: *Was it something you felt at Hillcroft?*

SALLY: It wasn't the same. That desperate feeling of frustration. I felt somewhat anxious here, standing on the edge of a cliff, waiting to descend and what I said to —— when I came back here last time, the first year was marvellous. The most marvellous of my life and, the second year I came here, I felt the whole atmosphere had changed. There was far more accent on passing exams and what we were going to go on to and so, as soon as I embarked on my second year, there was always that feeling of moving onto something else.

For adults who were still preoccupied with 'moving away from' the disjunctions they had experienced in their personal lives, and with surviving in the new environment, premature emphases on transition and the future may in themselves set up a particular kind of disjunction.

Learning contexts

A number spoke about how they would not have felt sufficient confidence to make their first encounter with higher education through the vehicle of distance learning. The theme of needing and wanting to learn in relation to others, as a means of building confidence, once again recurs in Vera's account. She was born a working-class woman in Australia but later experienced a largely middle-class life style and travel with her Oxbridge-educated husband. She returned to the Hillcroft course for career purposes, feeling at a loss with her children getting older. She later went on to do a degree at a polytechnic. Here, Vera describes how technology can play a role in meeting both needs, and she suggests that, having been successful at Hillcroft, and subsequently in her degree at a polytechnic where she effectively managed the disjunction she encountered, she might do future courses through distance learning. But she concedes that to have come back that way would have been, for her

too isolating. . . . I like bouncing off people and talking. Mind you, having done that once, I might find it easier to go on and do [a course] if I had to, like if we went abroad but the first experience. . . . So this is what video computers can do. Even if you can't see people, you can talk to them and see their faces. Interactive video. Tutors and three students linked over. Can see their faces on the screen. That seems to me there could be a big opportunity that must be taken. The technology is available and we ought to use it. So I would put the resources there.

For learners who have been away from the formal system for some time, and who left school with few if any qualifications, the route back seems to require active engagement with and support from others. Even Nina, a middle-class woman who had considerable experience of formal education throughout her life, speaks about how she would not wish to do a course in higher education if it were 'too large, which had too much of "up there". The "large" particularly and I want to be able to question and discuss. Those two things would be very important.'

Within the context of these needs, size of groups was a continual preoccupation, particularly in the accounts of adults whose prior experiences of learning, at school and for some at work, was one of feeling diminished by numbers. As Alex says, in relation to my question about her initial hopes for the degree course, she wanted

> stimulation. To develop confidence and a sense of achievement. To do some more substantial learning than the stuff you can get out of a book yourself. I wanted discussion, tutorial groups, interaction. Really to discuss things. And also status. All those around me were degreed people. I had done a three-year nurses' training but, because of the way I was treated in nursing, I felt like a little minion. I wanted confidence on the level my friends had. I didn't know if that came from the degree or them, but I wanted to find out.

Restructuring

Elsewhere, I have summarized the kinds of boundaries that were at issue for these learners (Weil 1988) and many of these are considered by Parry in Chapter 2 from a theoretical perspective. Here adults in the study speak about how they would restructure the system to enhance the quality of their own lifelong learning. A central preoccupation is how to make the resources of higher education available to people in new forms, and generally more accessible.

Access to knowledge, on one's own terms, is Janet's concern; she speaks about her interest in a particular subject, but how

> it has a way of keeping things from people. It is locked away from the average person. It's not that I am not up to it or not good enough. Whereas with art I knew little because ordinary people are kept out of it. But this is not the way it should be. It should be accessible. The history of art is different. Not everyone will want it. Like going to an art gallery, how many will enjoy it? But everyone has the capacity to enjoy it, but it is kept away from them. Education should be about introducing people to things versus keeping people out of things. It's like a nice club. Why, TV lets people into places where they otherwise wouldn't go. Now more is done for children.

Frank, as described previously, had encountered many barriers in the pursuit of his aspirations. His experience led him to believe that education needs to serve 'social purposes' and to be organized for the interests of a majority of people, and therefore the depth and breadth of learning would be different. There would be no sharp divisions between 'clever and less clever' but rather the emphasis would be on the development of potential. You could pursue various aspects of problems in ways which now, many are dulled. There would be no artificial boundaries between disciplines. The nature of the social and scientific problem would determine the structure and boundaries of knowledge.

Fran talks about how she would benefit from independent study, based on her encounter with a mature student who was doing such a programme. She and Georgette, whom I interviewed together, then explore this 'vision', in the course of which they reflect on the role of 'academic drift' in the polytechnic, and the tensions that students see operating on the part of staff:

FRAN: I could set up one of those tomorrow and get the students, and probably you could do the same. I would use project learning, anything I can get my hands on and, if they didn't know, I would teach them how to study, how to learn, how to use the books, and I would take a good term in making sure they understood how to go, where to get their information, how to use the system.
GEORGETTE: And monitor their progress all the time.
FRAN: All the way through.
GEORGETTE: Probably one individual who takes on another student as their special students and sees them through, so you are seeing people, and doing accurate monitoring, rather than this haphazard, uninvolved academic way. . . .
FRAN: I think the polytechnics can't make up their minds what they want to be, whether they want to be a university or. . . . Especially, on my course, they weren't sure. They weren't good enough to get the jobs in university. So they got the jobs in polytechnics and they try to run the system the same. Then they come up against the CNAA who won't let them run it like a university and this is their constant conflict. One wants to run it like a university would and the other half is wanting to do it different with the CNAA.
GEORGETTE: My son at school is always having to stand in a queue and that for me sums up what education is all about.

Todd has a similar vision in mind, when he speaks about the need for a higher-education system which is more the 'equivalent of a Citizens' Advice Bureau. Each person's problem is separate, but still there are broad categories. . . . So people will need to play a directional role and offer emotional support.'

Peter and Vera draw from their experiences, not as educationalists but as learners and members of this society, and consider the kinds of challenges and possibilities for positively transforming the system which wider access poses. Like so many in the study, there is a preoccupation with attitudinal and structural barriers, and the waste of potential that results from these.

Vera describes how, in her experience, class permeates the whole of the British educational system. As an outsider to this country who raised a family here, she vividly describes many of the barriers addressed by others in this book. After settling in Britain she first encountered the education system here in her role as a mother, and as the wife of someone who was formerly at Oxbridge. She identifies the roots of the problem in society, as well as in the premature emphasis on specialization and an overemphasis on academic achievement in schools:

SWW:*What would you like to see changed so it looked for people like yourself? [Going back] First time. Let's think the first time. Like you said.*
VERA: First time. Yes, because I didn't try to get into a British university. Like Cambridge or Oxford. How you make those listen, I don't know. A lot of it goes back in this country to the class structure, and I personally believe that a lot of problems in Britain can be put down to the whole class structure and that whole business of, in a way, early academic achievement. Such importance is laid. You know, if kids haven't achieved by the age of 14 or 15, they are not going to achieve. Therefore, they are channelled away from college and higher education altogether. I think that must be a mistake. I think if there was less importance put on early achievement, you would be likely to find that kids would achieve and want to go on. If it was automatic to assume you could go on to 18 without this great pressure of achievement at 15, 16. That's where I would like to see changes. . . . I think, a lot of people used to think, like my father did, long-haired louts go to university. I think that there still must be quite a bit of that and it is hard for working-class children to fight, and yet so many super brains come out of working-class families.

Peter, whose story has also been mentioned previously, implicitly deals with the issue of how increased learner responsibility and accountability might have long-term benefits. He also deals with the issue of student loans, but from a different value stance than the one customarily heard:

SWW: *Based on your experience of the formal system, and your own self-managed learning, are there ways in which you believe the system can be made more relevant to the needs of learners like yourself and if so, in what ways?*
PETER: Yes, there are, but they are quite revolutionary.
SWW: *Tell me a bit.*
PETER: First, students should have a say in how the course is structured. Quite a strong say, and I know that probably means that in the current educational system, they will decide to do as little as possible and stay stuck into space-invaders technology. But I think there would be a long-term pay off. I don't think people should be entitled to go to university and just waste three years. I think there should be more

control over whether the student is using this time properly. Like the
60s ideals. Of everyone having a right to education. Well, most
working-class people *never* have that opportunity and those that do
and are motivated should get full use of the resources, and all these
middle-class wallies wandering about doing nothing at university
should be chucked out as far as I am concerned. There isn't room for
them. And maybe one way of doing that is to make students pay for
their own education, so basically I agree with Keith Joseph, but for a
different reason. But they are not likely to pay for it unless they have
some say in its structure. The two need to go together. I don't think you
have to pay for it on the spot but afterwards. Sounds a bit hard, but I
am tired of listening to liberal people talking about wishy-washy
things. But these ideas don't work.

SWW: *Anything else about structure, process?*

PETER: There is too big a division between courses. I was just reading a
book recently, an historical book, and I was doing some research into
some fairly obscure historical things, and they were drawing on
legends, as a resource, mythology and archaeology and all these
things. Now, they were BBC investigative journalists doing this book.
They made a criticism there: that there is no way an historian would
have discovered this, but a literature student would have, and an
archaeologist would have, because it depended upon them having
cross-referenced all this stuff and taken up clues from one thing and
following them through to another, and they made a comment there
about our academic institutions being so divided up. Because there is
nothing but contempt between departments at university. We are the
guardians of the sole truth, and *this* is the only way of looking at
things. . . . And that fascinates me because they are not prepared to
listen to perspectives on other subjects.

Widening access

When I began this study, I was convinced that progressive teaching and
learning methods and approaches were the key to responding effectively to
the demands to be placed on higher education by wider access. Student-
centredness, experiential learning, andragogy, and group processes were
the touchstones around which I evolved my own professional practice (see
Weil and McGill 1989). This systematic inquiry, however, challenged me to
think about education and higher education and the experience of
learning, from altogether new and more elaborated perspectives. I began
to scrutinize my perhaps idealistic assumptions about the process and
impact of education and higher education. Certain taken-for-granted
assumptions, once made explicit, took a bruising. I began to question many
of the normative assumptions from psychology and about adult learning
that permeate the literature and conventional wisdom about adults as

learners (see also Tennant 1988). I realized the extent to which wider access would pose fundamental challenges to traditional staff, subject and sector boundaries in higher education (Schuller, Tight and Weil 1988).

The subtleties and complexities of the struggles conveyed in these adults' stories defy broad and easy generalizations. For such learners, the different aspects of their learning situation that we so easily separate for the purposes of research or of cogent argument about access are inextricably interrelated. All at once adult learners are involved in relationships with the following:

● with staff who will differ greatly in their personal stances towards different kinds of students, and towards process concerns;
● with a particular programme and the complexities of an area of academic study;
● with varying priorities and approaches either at odds with or congruent with their entering concerns and expectations;
● with implicit values and meanings deeply embedded in the histories and cultures of particular disciplines, departments and institutions;
● with different languages and assumptions about education and learning.

The cumulative effect of these experiences can give rise to an *overall* sense of disjunction or integration on the part of learners. There seems to be a certain kind of integrity to an individual learner's lived experience that defies reductionism. I believe that these learners raise important questions about the validity of treating as separate problems the issues of impact and process; of institutional structures and culture; of student and staff experience. It would seem that a commitment to wider access needs to rest on an acknowledgement of just how 'all of a piece' these are, particularly from the perspective of learners who enter higher and continuing education feeling *not* 'all of a piece' because of their earlier experiences of learning, whether within or outside formal education. It would seem that our considerations of quality and responsiveness and, indeed, even the notion of 'potential to benefit' need to respect this integrity and inter-relatedness.

Thus, as far as wider access is concerned, we may not be able to wrest easily the experience of being a learner, and learning in an academic environment, from concerns with personal and social identity, personal and social context, and the notion of integration or disjunction. A disenfranchised adult learner with a particular learning history may experience a profound sense of disjunction upon entry, for example, in reaction to the messages conveyed by the structure of the classrooms, or the attitudes and procedures encountered during the admission and orientation stages of engaging with an institution. Alternatively, low self-esteem and the sense that one does not 'really belong here' can quickly be brought to the surface by the attitude of a tutor who regards prior experience as of little value, or by someone who briskly or impatiently urges someone to speak up. Another may feel undermined by an encounter with a teacher who, like a woman's husband, quietly thinks that the emphasis women might place on the interpretation of connections within the whole, and on interrelationships, is slightly suspect on a science course. Her interventions, her attempts to make sense of the subject within her world view, may continually remain quietly and politely unrecognized and kept invisible until, without watering, attempts to speak wither and die.

On the other hand, positively to emphasize prior experience and to encourage a greater degree of learner responsibility and accountability may set up fundamental disjunctions, also involving issues of personal and social identity, for those who have been socialized into another mode of operating within formal education. A certain quality of relationships may be required to help a learner whose prior sense of integration in formal learning has been dependent largely upon taken-for-granted attitudes, assumptions and practices. The quality of relationships and dialogue will be vital to effecting a shift to, for example, a situation where deep rather than surface learning becomes more possible or where greater learner responsibility and accountability are welcomed.

Moreover, these learners have conveyed powerful images of how progressive teaching and learning approaches cannot counteract in themselves the ethos of an institution, the wider social context in which learning takes place, and the structures which may strangle possibilities for learning despite the genuine efforts of teachers and learners working in partnership to evolve a different reality. Alternatively, the tacit messages sent out by, for example, an absence of women within a departmental staff group or the disabling attitudes on the part of some teachers, whom one cannot avoid in certain programmes, may be experienced by some learners as yet another obstacle that impedes the possibility of learning and education in that situation.

Rescrutinizing wider-access 'solutions'

Access courses, modular programmes and distance or open learning are often held up as the 'solution' to wider access. I should like to reflect on each of these in turn, drawing on the perspectives and experiences of learners in this study.

Distance or open learning

A significant pattern throughout the literature on the characteristics of adult learners who participate in higher and continuing education is that those who have had the most previous education are most likely to participate (e.g. OECD 1987; Woodley 1987 *et al.*). But when we consider the experience of learning in higher and continuing education from the alternative perspectives of adults in this study, the limitations of building-block models of learning, which can underpin distance teaching modes, become more apparent. Salmon, drawing on Piaget, argues instead that 'Intellectual progression does not entail knowing more, rather it is a matter of knowing differently' (Salmon 1988: 72, after Piaget 1958). She goes on to suggest that

> the process is not one of steady incremental progression. It takes a far more wayward course, often descending into total confusion, and lurching into grossly oversimplified formulations. And what is critical, apparently, for movement forward, is that our present ways of understanding things can be put to the test, opened up to validational outcomes. Only if what we think we know can somehow be challenged, and events made to yield evidence as to its validity, its fertility, is it possible to take things further – to learn.
>
> (Salmon 1988: 77)

What these learners emphasize is the extent to which personal support, personal encouragement and personal valuing, and learning-in-relation create the possibility for developing new ways of understanding things, for putting things genuinely to a test, for opening up present ideas to alternative scrutiny, and thus for education. In this kind of context, the disjunction that can arise out of the kind of invalidation of which Salmon speaks becomes not disabling, but integral to the process of significant learning and intellectual progression itself.

For those learners who have never consciously felt their personal and social identity to be at risk in formal education, and who enter learning situations with a clear 'moving-toward' orientation, perhaps an instrumental approach to a building-block model of learning can be sustained by the learner to some extent, through distance- and open-learning modes. I have little doubt that these approaches will benefit many adult learners. But do they not cater almost exclusively for those who have had a great deal of previous experience of education characterized overall by a sense of integration? I question their appropriateness for learners with low self-esteem who have largely experienced disjunction in their interactions with formal education.

Access courses

Access courses are also often proposed as 'the solution' to attracting new groups of students. The effectiveness of many access initiatives at present rests in their emphasis on, and the quality of, their relationships and process (Woodrow 1988; see also Chapters 2 and 4). They tend to be targeted at groups of previously disenfranchised learners and explicitly value and build upon the meanings and perceptions arising from their life world (Wildemeersch 1989). This study suggests that the experience of such situations, when characterized overall by a sense of integration, can also provide less confident learners with a valuable store of confidence on which to draw when confronted with different kinds of learning environments.

I fear, however, that it is the students, rather than the institutions, who carry the burden of responsibility for managing disjunction, if their subsequent transition to higher education involves them in a disabling, rather than an enabling, situation.

My involvement in this study causes me to favour a determined move towards the situation where institutions, departments, course designers, tutors and students are accountable and responsible for creating and sustaining enabling environments which, as a whole, promote academic excellence as well as a sense of integration for the diverse kinds of learners who participate within them. By this I do not mean to imply that Access courses should be replaced, although I do fear their institutionalization as the 500-hour hurdle on the way to higher education (CNAA 1989). I believe they can be an important force for change. But greater responsibility and accountability within higher education itself for promoting continuity rather than discontinuity seem essential. Learners from Access courses will increasingly expect certain kinds of emphases and processes to be integral to the experience of academic programmes generally. To fail in this can only increase the likelihood of disjunction for new kinds of learners – who may be attracted but not retained.

It would seem there needs to be greater investment of time and human resources in opportunities that promote learning-in-relation and favour a particular kind of ongoing dialogue and reflection on the experience of that course and learning in that environment. This study supports the vital role played by there being ample space for support, challenge, the teasing out of meaning and experience, and the nurturing of relationships that enhance the possibility of education rather than miseducation. The responsibility to consider learners' needs, as whole people, managing a complex learning environment, needs to rest with all teachers generally, and with some teachers specifically – but not solely with the counselling and support services often set up to 'help' mature students.

Space for learning implies opportunities to reflect on individual and collective goals, within the boundaries and possibilities of a particular programme or subject area. Enabling teachers and groups can go a long way to counteract the impact of disjunction arising from forces that seem outside the bounds of one person's agency, and to create an oasis of integration in which the experience of other kinds of disjunction can be made sense of and more effectively managed.

In addition, regular orientation programmes and events could involve staff and students alike in planning for and reflecting upon their experience of learning together, both generally and, as appropriate, specifically within the framework of that discipline (as in the ways suggested by Ramsden 1987). Such events could provide a more organic approach to staff development, since they encourage ongoing reflection-on-action (Schon 1983), while also giving staff greater access to learners' meanings and perceptions (see also Gibbs 1981; Ramsden 1987). Such kinds of activities emphasize quality as a dynamic, rather than a static, feature of learning environments, in which all players are responsible and accountable.

Perhaps staff development should be most concerned with feeding back the outcomes of learner-centred studies to tutors and students as a basis for evolving a common language through which they can learn from their experiences of learning and together enhance the quality of a particular programme in every respect.

Modular programmes

A reframing of our priorities, our use of resources, and the balance of process and content concerns in courses would also seem to be vital to the success of modular programmes. At present, the notion of a 'core module' tends to refer to content priorities. But it is in process considerations that the key to the development of potential seems to lie. Perhaps we need to consider modular programmes in which learners can pick and choose content-oriented modules (which in themselves should also be addressing issues of process), but the 'honeycomb' which holds it together consists of the core-process strands.

Core-process strands can involve students in identifying goals and planning how to use resources within the learning environment and in the community. Within this context, lectures serve as valuable resources to be used within the context of students' emergent goals, interests and priorities. Such strands could require students to come together with students from other disciplines. Self and peer assessment approaches can be used to evaluate the effectiveness with which individuals and groups explain their values, their learning insights and outcomes, and the coherence that they derive from their programmes of study.

In such modules, the legitimacy of reflecting upon and learning from their experiences can be upheld. Moreover, to communicate the experience of one's distinctive pathway to others, and the excitement and enthusiasm for what one is doing, in the context of who one is, where one has been and may be going, can be a powerful motivator, as is evident in the interviews from this study. Moreover, important skills are developed in the course of having to explain oneself to others who do not necessarily share their experience.

Such activities, if made integral as the key strands in modular programmes, to support the use of the 'content modules' to full advantage, would address the concerns of a number of new stakeholders in higher education. Such modules could improve communication skills across personal and subject-based meaning structures – a major concern to industry. Core-process modules on modular programmes can also provide opportunities for students to engage in structured cycles of learning that enable them to reflect upon and plan for learning experiences that will

increase their sense of integration within their programme; to con-
ceptualize and make links with existing theory and research, and plan for
applying learning insights and outcomes in new kinds of situations (for
example, see Cowan 1988). Such cycles of learning can develop not just
academic potential, but also learners' potential to work with others, to
identify problems, to effect change, and to learn how to learn.

Conclusion

Adult learners do not bring their experience with them into education;
they *are* their experience (Knowles 1978). But the answers to the real
complexities and challenges of this idea do not seem to lie simply in
modular programmes, access courses, distance- or open-learning initiatives, experiential learning or andragogy. They lie in much finer nuances
of expressing respect, concern and care for individuals, and in giving
priority to the need for adults to build upon and make sense of their
experiences within the context of their own and others' 'life worlds'
(Wildemeersch 1989).

Issues crucial to wider access – such as impact and process, boundaries
and partnerships and institutional structures – gain in meaning when they
are examined from the perspective of learners who, in their bones, can feel
the interrelatedness of these dimensions to their experience of learning in
higher and continuing education. Moreover, probably better than any of us
they can see if and when the Emperor has no clothes:

> People may find it hard to accept that their personal models are not the
> world as it is but are constructed realities and they are not soundly
> based in absolute truths. When faced with the challenge of [alternative
> views], people may be unwilling to accept the responsibility which goes
> along with the acknowledgement that it is *they* that construct their own
> world views. For many, it is more acceptable to believe that their worlds
> are imposed upon them by the way things really are.
>
> (Pope 1985: 5)

We can dismiss the issues arising from such studies as 'culpably
subjective' and 'dangerously subversive' (Kelly 1970). But maybe the
experience in the USA can alert us to some of the consequences that lurk
around future corners, should we decide to do so. There attention is
increasingly being focused on attrition, retention, and on new meanings of
quality and good practice, rather than merely on access (Astin 1975; Beal
and Noel 1980; Boyer 1986; Levitz and Noel 1986; Tinto 1986).

These adults present us with the opportunity to raise fundamental
questions about quality and responsiveness from perspectives entirely
different from those that usually figure in such debates. For example, to
what extent and why do we feel able to assure new kinds of learners of the
possibility of education, not miseducation? How do we *know* if we offer to

new kinds of students an education that enables, rather than compounds, previous disabling forces? What more do we need to do, and which of our many strengths do we most need to build upon? How can existing resources be used in alternative ways, in order, as Wright says (Chapter 7) to put learning at the heart of our academic institutions?

In these adults' stories, we find the clues as to the kinds of issues we need to address if we are to ensure that wider access remains concerned with more and different students (not just more and the same) and quality for all. By reframing the problems, and by exploring alternative solutions, we may very well create new kinds of pathways to enable those of us in higher education to move with integrity and greater clarity through what may now seem only a tangled thicket of demands from too many stakeholders. And in so doing, many other adults may approach our doorways, confident that here we do not just imagine the future, but here the future is lived.

References

Arthur, C. (1988) 'Off target shots in the dark' in *Times Higher Education Supplement*, 23 December 1988, p. 11.

Aslanian, C. B. and Brickell, H. M. (1980) *Americans in Transition: Life Changes as a Reason for Learning*, Princeton, New Jersey, College Entrance Examination Board.

Astin, A. W. (1975) *Preventing Students from Dropping Out*, San Francisco, Jossey Bass.

Ball, C. (1988) 'What is the use of higher education?', address delivered at University of St Andrews, 23 February 1988.

Beal, P. E. and Noel, L. (1980) *What Works in Student Retention*, Iowa City, American College Testing Programme.

Boyer, E. (1986) 'College: the undergraduate experience in America', Washington D.C., Carnegie Foundation for the Advancement of Teaching.

Brookfield, S. (1986) *Understanding and Facilitating Adult Learning*, Milton Keynes, Open University Press.

Council for National Academic Awards (1989) *Access Courses to Higher Education: A Framework of National Arrangements for Recognition*, London, Council for National Academic Awards and Committee of Vice-Chancellors and Principals.

Cowan, J. (1988) 'A model of experiential learning and its facilitation' in Candy, R. and Jaques, D. (eds) *Learning for Action: Course Development for Capability in Higher Education*, Standing Conference on Educational Development, Occasional Paper No. 51.

Chickering, A. W. (1981) *The Modern American College: Responding to the New Realities of Diverse Students in a Changing Society*, San Francisco, Jossey Bass.

Dewey, J. (1938) *Experience and Education*, New York, Collier.

Entwistle, N. and Ramsden, P. (1983) *Understanding Student Learning*, London, Croom Helm.

Gibbs, G. (1981) *Teaching Students to Learn: A Student Centred Approach*, Milton Keynes, Open University Press.

Jarvis, P. (1987) *Adult Learning in the Social Context*, London, Croom Helm.

Kelly, G. A. (1970) 'A brief introduction to Personal Construct Theory', in Bannister D. (ed.) *Perspectives in Personal Construct Theory*, London, Academic Press.

Knowles, M. (1978) *The Adult Learner: a Neglected Species*, Houston, Texas, Gulf Publishing Company.

Levitz, R. and Noel, L. (1986) 'Using a systematic approach to assessing retention needs', in Noel, L. and Levitz, R. (eds) *Increasing Student Retention*, San Francisco, Jossey Bass.

Marton, F., Hounsell, D. and Entwistle, N. (1984) *The Experience of Learning*, Edinburgh, Scottish Academic Press.

Mezirow, J. (1978) 'Perspective transformation', *Adult Education* (US) 38 (2), 100–10.

Mezirow, J. (1985) 'Concept and action in adult education', *Adult Education Quarterly* (US) 35 (3), 142–51.

National Advisory Body (1984) *Report of the Continuing Education Group*, London, National Advisory Body.

Noel, L. and Levitz, R. (1986) *Increasing Student Retention*, San Francisco, Jossey Bass.

Organization for Economic Co-operation and Development (1987) *Adults in Higher Education*, Paris, Centre for Educational Research and Innovation.

Perry, W. (1981) 'Cognitive and ethical growth: the making of meaning' in Chickering, A. *et al.* (1981) *The Modern American College*, San Francisco, Jossey Bass.

Perry, W. (1989) 'Different worlds in the same classroom' in Ramsden, P. (ed.) *Improving Learning*, London, Kogan Page.

Piaget, J. (1958) *The Child's Construction of Reality*, London, Routledge and Kegan Paul.

Pope, M. (1985) 'Constructivist goggles: implications for process in teaching and learning', paper presented at BERA Conference, Sheffield.

Ramsden, P. (1987) 'Improving teaching and learning: the case for a relational perspective', *Studies in Higher Education*, 12 (3), 275–86.

Ramsden, P. (ed.) (1988) *Improving Learning: New Perspectives*, London, Kogan Page.

Richardson, J., Eysenck, M. W. and Warren Piper, D. W. (eds) (1987) *Student Learning*, Milton Keynes, SRHE and Open University Press.

Salmon, P. (1988) *Psychology for Teachers: An Alternative Approach*, London, Hutchinson.

Salmon, P. (1989) 'Personal stances in learning' in Weil, S. W. and McGill, I. (eds) *Making Sense of Experiential Learning: Diversity in Theory and Practice*, Milton Keynes, SRHE and Open University Press.

Schon, D. (1983) *The Reflective Practitioner: How Professionals Think in Action*, London, Temple Smith.

Schuller, T., Tight, M. and Weil, S. (1988) 'Continuing education and the redrawing of boundaries', *Higher Education Quarterly*, 42 (4), 335–52.

Taylor, M. (1986) 'Learning for self-direction in the classroom: the pattern of a transition process', *Studies in Higher Education*, 11 (1), 55–72.

Tennant, M. (1988) *Psychology and Adult Learning*, London, Routledge and Kegan Paul.

Tinto, V. (1986) 'Dropping out and other forms of withdrawal from college', in Noel, L. and Levitz, R. (eds) *Increasing Student Retention*, San Francisco, Jossey Bass.

University Grants Committee (1984) *Report of the Continuing Education Working Party*, London, HMSO.

Weil, S. (1986) 'Non-traditional students in traditional higher education institutions: discovery and disappointment', *Studies in Higher Education*, 11 (3), 219–35.

Weil, S. W. (1988) 'From a language of observation to a language of experience: studying the perspectives of diverse adults in higher education', *Journal of Access Studies*, 3 (1), 17–43.

Weil, S. W. and McGill, I. (1989) 'A framework for making sense of experiential learning' in Weil, S. W. and McGill, I. (eds) *Making Sense of Experiential Learning: Diversity in Theory and Practice*, Milton Keynes, SRHE and Open University Press.

Weil, S. W. and McGill, I. (1989) *Making Sense of Experiential Learning: Diversity in Theory and Practice*, Milton Keynes, SRHE and Open University Press.

Wildemeersch, D. (1989) 'The principal meaning of dialogue for the construction and transformation of reality' in Weil, S. W. and McGill, I. (eds) *Making Sense of Experiential Learning: Diversity in Theory and Practice*, Milton Keynes, SRHE and Open University Press.

Woodley, A., Wagner, L., Slowey, M., Hamilton, M. and Fulton, O. (1987) *Choosing to Learn: Adults in Education*, Milton Keynes, SRHE and Open University Press.

Woodrow, M. (1988) 'The access route to higher education' in *Higher Education Quarterly*, 42 (4).

Part 3

Institutional Change

9

National Policy and Institutional Development

Leslie Wagner

The delivery of access, as with most things in higher education, ultimately depends on the behaviour of the institutions themselves. It is the policies and practices of polytechnics, colleges and universities on recruitment, admissions, course structures, curriculum, pedagogy and student facilities which will primarily determine their degree of success in widening access.

The power of governments and funding bodies to influence or to determine institutional behaviour can be both enormously strong and remarkably weak. Governments find it easier to prevent than to promote, but they prefer to exhort rather than to compel. How then have government and the funding bodies approached the issue of access through the 1980s and what are the prospects for the 1990s?

Instruments for action

The instruments available to government (and the funding bodies – we shall use the two interchangeably in this chapter) are in ascending order of imperative strength: encouragement and exhortation; financial incentives and penalties (carrots and sticks); and legislative order.

Encouragement and exhortation are the most frequently used tools of government policy. They appear in every ministerial speech, whether in Parliament or outside, and in the utterances of funding-body chairmen and chief executives. They are the staple diet of working-group and official reports and the essential discourse of higher education policy.

In most cases each statement is simply part of a series all within the framework of a particular policy direction, such as yet another speech from the Minister for Higher Education saying unit costs must fall, or that the government is committed to quality. But, in other cases, statements can be seen at the time or in retrospect as having produced a seminal shift in policy and in attitudes. The famous Robbins axiom of 1963 that courses 'should be available for all those qualified by ability and attainment to pursue them' comes into this category.

Encouragement and exhortation are the weakest policy weapons. At the lowest level they are simply rhetoric – meaningless statements without commitment. Yet they can also be the most powerful, establishing the intellectual and political climate within which policy is discussed, formulated and refined. A well-timed and articulately phrased statement can have a significant impact. It will provide a clear sense of direction. Those institutions already sympathetic to the view expressed will be encouraged and stimulated to continue, feeling virtuous and loved (an underestimated motivating power at all levels of management). Those apathetic or opposed will have reason to pause and to re-assess the possibilities of avoiding the need to move in the direction indicated.

From the government's point of view, the most useful and powerful statements are those which induce institutions to change their behaviour without the need for financial incentive or other action. Rhetoric is not to be underestimated. It is always a necessary and sometimes a sufficient agent for change. No significant shift in policy takes place without the adoption and assimilation first of the rhetoric.

Financial incentives and penalties are, of course, more direct in their impact on institutional behaviour, but are usually used cautiously. One reason, inevitably, is that the use of a financial incentive will increase public expenditure. Governments (or at least the Treasury) will always ask whether the expenditure is necessary and whether, in particular, the desired change could not be brought about by some other means. Why use money when you may not need to? More seriously, it is difficult to target incentives so that they have an impact precisely on the area intended. This is, of course, one of the arguments used against general welfare benefits. And, even more seriously, it can be argued that some financial incentives can have a perverse impact producing an effect the opposite of what was intended. An example will be given later.

To some extent, a disincentive is the mirror image of an incentive. Fees paid by students on part-time courses can be seen as encouraging or discouraging participation, depending on the level at which they are fixed. Some recent examples of financial incentives used to deliver policies in higher education are the early-retirement schemes to encourage the appointment of 'new blood', and the HITECC programme to encourage institutions to provide conversion courses into engineering for those without the necessary qualifications. The most obvious use of a financial disincentive in pursuit of a stated policy during the 1980s was the establishment of full-cost fees for overseas students.

The use of *law* enables government to use compulsion to implement its policies. Where exhortation and incentive have failed, the law will succeed. Or will it? In some cases the answer is obviously, yes. The Education Reform Act removed the control of the polytechnics from local education authorities after the government concluded that the exhortation it had practised and the financial and national planning arrangements it had introduced in the early 1980s had not produced sufficient movement in the directions it wished. Moreover, in setting up the new higher-education corporations the government has not used exhortation to persuade the polytechnics to provide a majority of their new governing bodies from the world of employment. The new Act compels them to do so. The same Act provides for the removal of automatic academic tenure for new appointments in the universities. Exhortation to move in this direction during the preceding years was deemed by the government to be insufficient.

The law is best used in setting the framework and the context to influence behaviour. It is less useful in compelling the behaviour directly. For example, a large number of business people on a court of governors may produce a more efficient operation in time. The greater efficiency, however, cannot be legislated for. A financial discentive is likely to be a much more powerful tool of policy to achieve this objective.

Access and national policy

How have these different instruments of policy-making been used by governments and funding bodies during the 1980s in relation to access, and what has been their effect on institutional behaviour? The past decade is best divided into three periods: 1978–83; 1984–6; and 1987 to the present.

1978–83

The decade began with two government documents at the end of the 1970s looking at the impact of the projections of an increasing 18-year-old population in the early 1980s, followed by a rapid decline in the second half of the decade (Department of Education and Science (DES) 1978, 1979).

The first document offered five alternative approaches to coping with the demographic changes, including the famous 'Model E' which allowed for a substantial increase in numbers to cover both the increase in 18-year-olds and wider access. Those in higher education rushed to advocate the adoption of Model E, marrying as always self-interest with public interest. In those 'golden' days it was assumed that increased numbers meant more or less pro-rata increased finance. A golden period for higher education beckoned.

The government (and it was a Labour government) was not so easily persuaded. Model E was a vision that turned into a mirage and it soon became clear that the immediate need as far as government was concerned was to find ways of 'tunnelling through the hump', i.e. to allow a steady increase in numbers to reflect the increasing demand of the early 1980s but not to commit pro-rata resources. The rhetoric was about constraints.

However, while publicly the immediate concern was to hold the line against an excessive demographic-induced expansion, behind the scenes more longer-term planning was taking place. In 1978 the first government recognition of access courses occurred when the DES invited selected local authorities to provide Access Studies to higher education. By 1984 130 such courses had been identified (Lucas and Ward 1985).

In 1979 the Department recognized its need to understand better the extent of and reasons for mature-student participation in education, in preparation for the downturn in 18-year-old participation then expected in the mid-1980s. Instead of waiting for research projects to be suggested, it invited researchers in this area to submit proposals to meet the objectives which the Department itself set down for the research. The work was concluded and made available to the Department in 1983 and was eventually published in 1987 (Woodley *et al.* 1987).

On the surface, however, the mood was one of, at best, containment and, at worst, retrenchment. This was encapsulated in two financial signals of disincentive to expansion which had completely different effects. The funds to the universities were reduced in 1981 and the University Grants Committee (UGC), in response, reduced the funds and the target numbers for individual universities. The government subsequently disassociated itself from the furore surrounding the differential impact of these reductions on particular universities, but the general impact was a good example of a financial disincentive working through quickly into institutional behaviour.

The government intended the same change to occur in the polytechnics but the outcome was somewhat different. In part, this was due to the financial instruments available. The funding of the polytechnics and colleges within the local-authority system occurred through an arcane pooling methodology in which (basically) local authorities and their institutions received funding at an agreed unit rate on the basis of their enrolled students in the previous year. As most of the overall bill was picked up by central government, it was a direct incentive to expansion. The more students enrolled, the more money was received. With this system in operation, the financial implications of the demographic expansion of the early 1980s looked horrendous to the incoming Conservative government, pledged to reduce public expenditure.

The financial instrument used by the DES to constrain this growth was the capping of the pool. The theory was simple. Instead of the bill being open-ended and thus providing institutions with the incentive to take more and more students, the government would fix its total bill in advance. Institutions would then know that the consequence of taking more students would be not more money but reduced unit costs. Enlightened self-interest would ensure that numbers were restrained.

It didn't happen. In part this was because many institutions did not assimilate or understand the new rules; in part it was due to a time-lag. With funding in any year being dependent on numbers a year or two earlier, the capping of the pool in its earlier years had to be relatively generous to allow for the earlier expansion. The impact on institutional finances was not as immediate as with the universities.

More fundamentally, the system itself had an inherent flaw. The only change was that the total funds to be distributed were now fixed. The basis for distribution was still the numbers enrolled in a previous year. As long as institutions agreed collectively not to increase numbers beyond that allowed for by the funding provided, none would be worse off. But there was no mechanism for ensuring that this collective decision occurred. Each institution acted individually and the key to financial improvement was to ensure that your own enrolment increase was above the average for the sector. However, no one knew what the average increase would be so the safest policy was to expand as fast as possible. Of course, unit costs would fall, but for an individual polytechnic they'd fall even more if other institutions had expanded and it had not. The capping of the pool was a prime example of a policy instrument which did not work and of a situation where the aggregate of individual decisions did not produce a sensible collective decision.

The DES saw the implications of such a policy early enough and in 1982 the National Advisory Body for Local Authority Higher Education (NAB) was established to plan student numbers against funding. However, it was 1984 before it could bring its planning system into operation and the early years of the 1980s saw an unprecedented expansion of student numbers and a reduction in unit costs in the polytechnics and colleges. The students denied places in the universities by the UGC 1981 decision flocked to the polytechnics which, driven by the dynamics of the capped pooling system, were delighted to accept them. As a result of the expanded intakes of 1981–3, overall numbers increased significantly to the middle of the decade, even with the NAB's valiant efforts to hold intakes steady from 1984 onwards. In the first half of the decade numbers increased by nearly 30 per cent and unit costs fell by nearly twenty-five per cent in the polytechnics and colleges – a marvellous expansion of access but hardly what had been intended by the financial systems introduced. None of this, of course, prevented the government from taking credit for the expansion after it had occurred.

1984–6

The work of the NAB and the UGC were important in changing the rhetoric of higher education in favour of access during the 1980s. The NAB had the difficult task of attempting to restrict numbers in the immediate future, on the grounds that unit costs had fallen far enough and increased numbers required increased finance, while simultaneously arguing the longer-term case for an increase in access. Both it and the UGC used similar instruments for this exercise in encouragement and exhortation – the reports of their respective Continuing Education Working Groups and the publication of their longer-term strategies for higher education. All four reports appeared in 1984 and, collectively, they changed the climate for access and continuing education.

The Continuing Education reports were comprehensive documents reviewing existing provision, arguing the case for expansion and setting down the changes necessary to enable the expansion to take place. In many cases the proposals were in the classic exhortatory mode, addressed to institutions and urging them to change their behaviour to make themselves welcoming to non-traditional students. Other proposals urged the funding bodies to continue the exhortation and pressure through, for example, monitoring of performance. A further set of proposals went beyond exhortation and identified financial incentives to promote access.

The theme of promoting continuing education was taken forward into the strategy documents of the two funding bodies. The impact was strengthened by their agreement to publish a joint chapter on the purpose of higher education which included the following statements on continuing education:

> Continuing education needs to be fostered not only for its essential role in promoting economic prosperity but also for its contribution to personal development and social progress. It can renew personal confidence, regenerate the human spirit and restore a sense of purpose to people's lives through the cultivation of new interests. In short, both effective economic performance and harmonious social relationships depend on our ability to deal successfully with the changes and uncertainties which are now ever present in our personal and working lives. This is the primary role which we see for continuing education.
> (University Grants Committee 1984b; National Advisory Body 1984b)

More dramatically, the chapter proposed a fifth objective for higher education to stand alongside the four set out in the Robbins Report some twenty years earlier, namely: 'the provision of continuing education in order to facilitate adjustment to technological, economic and social change and to meet individual needs for personal development'.

The NAB/UGC Strategy Chapter also addressed the question of access in the following terms:

> We re-affirm the importance of access and the provision of opportunity. However, the Robbins axiom should be interpreted as broadly as possible particularly in relation to the term 'qualified'. Essentially a student's qualification is used to form a judgement on his or her ability to benefit from a course. Yet evidence shows that school examinations such as A levels are not always good predictors of achievement in

higher education and that other qualities and experience can be important determinants of success. We believe that the Robbins axiom is more appropriately re-stated as 'courses of higher education should be available for all those who are able to benefit from them and who wish to do so'.

This position had been anticipated by the Council for National Academic Awards which in 1980 had issued a statement on the extension of access to higher education. The statement observed: 'the key point is that all applicants should be judged on their individual merits in the light of their total educational background and experience in relation to the demands of the particular course for which they have applied.' The statement pointed out that, 'provided they are satisfied that the students have the necessary motivation, potential and knowledge to follow the course successfully', institutions have discretion to admit mature students without formal qualifications.

The government's response to the strategy documents of the funding bodies came in 1985 with the publication of its Green Paper *The Development of Higher Education into the 1990s* (Department of Education and Science 1985). Its general tone was depressing for those in higher education with its emphasis on the need for greater efficiency and a seeming concern for an élitist concept of quality. However, the Green Paper did include separate chapters on access and continuing education.

The chapter on access grudgingly accepted the NAB/UGC advice on 'ability to benefit' and explained its understanding of the phrase in the following terms: 'The intellectual competence, motivation and maturity of the student should be consistent with the course, which must itself be of a standard appropriate to higher education.' The caveat that 'the benefit has to justify the cost' was also added. The chapter on continuing education was more positive, accepting that 'the provision of continuing education should be one of the principal parts of higher education work' and that the government 'should give the lead in promoting it'. However, government finance was to be strictly limited and it was up to employers and students themselves to pay for the bulk of the costs of the courses that met their needs and from which they benefited.

1987–9

The Keith Joseph caveat about benefits having to be greater than costs does not appear in the 1987 White Paper produced by Kenneth Baker. Indeed, the document widens the criteria for entry even further by using the phrase 'places should be available for all with the necessary *qualities* to benefit from higher education'. The use of the word 'qualities' rather than 'qualification' is a significant change indicating that the judgement of an individual's ability to benefit from higher education should be based on more than academic qualifications. Moreover, the statement comes at the head of a section entitled 'Widening access' which discusses approvingly routes into higher education other than A levels.

Ministerial speeches during 1988 and into 1989 regularly emphasized the importance of access. For example, in April 1988 Robert Jackson, speaking to a conference at the Royal Society declared:

> Women, black people and children from manual workers' homes are all underrepresented in higher education. Unequal access is not just uneconomic but unfair and unjust as well. A society which is both stable and dynamic requires able people from every background to have access to its institutions of higher education.

Later that year the NAB, in its final work before its abolition, published the report of its Equal Opportunities Working Group entitled *Action for Access*. It is a wide-ranging report focusing on the importance of equal opportunities as integral to access. There are 47 recommendations, most of which are exhortatory, calling for changes in behaviour, mostly by institutions, although there are some proposals also for financial incentives.

In a keynote speech at Lancaster University in January 1989 the Secretary of State for Education and Science urged as follows:

> We have already indicated our intention that, notwithstanding the fall in the number of 18-year-olds, the numbers in higher education should be sustained in the mid-1990s. The evidence to date is that we shall succeed in this. To do so means that we will have substantially to increase the participation rate among 18-year-olds – from nearly 15 per cent at present to something approaching 20 per cent.
>
> We are embarked on vitally important groundwork now. When the number of 18-year-olds starts to rise again in the latter part of the 1990s, the whole of higher education will be poised to expand on the basis both of this increased participation from the conventional student age group, and of new patterns of recruitment among non-conventional students.

The cynic may say that these are merely fine words as yet unsupported by financial help. It can also be argued that the gradual but sustained shift to an access policy has been motivated by instrumentalist reasons. For just as demography required the hump to be tunnelled at the beginning of the decade, it now requires the valley to be bridged. Our economic well-being now requires more qualified personnel to be available and so access is temporarily in favour.

All this may be true but it does not change the lesson that rhetoric, whatever its underlying motivation, is not to be underestimated. As a result of these various statements, there has been a change in the climate within which access is discussed and implemented at every level: government, funding bodies, and institutions. Access has become central not marginal; legitimate not sinful; and internal not external to higher education.

Finance

Rhetoric may be important but it cannot on its own stimulate access. To what extent has it been backed up by finance? Or, to put it more colloquially, has government put its money where its mouth is?

For central government the answer is, largely, no. The expansion of numbers in the polytechnics in the first half of the 1980s was not matched by increased funding. As has already been indicated, unit costs fell by nearly twenty-five per cent. On the other hand, the lack of funding did not seem to deter the institutions unduly as they consistently recruited above the targets set by the NAB. From the government's point of view, there seemed little point in providing additional funds for something that was happening anyway. Or, as a well-known polytechnic director at the time put it: 'You don't put corn in the hen house when the chicken's already in the oven.' On more specific areas of finance there has been some success. One issue during the 1980s has been the funding provided for part-time students. In the universities sector the methodology has been relatively simple and non-controversial. The standard full-time degree course takes three years and, if a part-time degree course takes five years, then in any year a part-time student is counted as 0.6 of a full-time equivalent. Given the homogeneity of university provision, a pro-rata approach made sense. One difficulty emerged in relation to Birkbeck College. In recognition of the fact that it was a wholly part-time institution, it had traditionally received a higher weighting for its students to reflect the greater burden of overheads which in another institution might be covered by the full-time student funding. In 1986 this was threatened by a changed formula from the UGC and London University which reduced the funding provided. However, after a vigorous campaign, arrangements were made which, while not retaining the status quo, allowed a longer period of adjustment.

In the polytechnics and colleges sector matters were more complex and therefore more difficult. There is no standardized course. Part-time provision ranges from the five-year degree course (à la universities) and two- or three-year part-time postgraduate courses, through one-day-plus-evening day-release courses (usually for a BTEC or professional certificate), to one-evening-a-week courses often held in local further-education colleges. To produce some order from this diversity, the funding formula simply distinguished between day students and evening students. Monitoring of the attendance of day students led to the adoption of a formula of 0.4 of a full-time equivalent for funding purposes and this was generally accepted. The funding formula for evening students, based on monitoring attendance, was fixed at 0.2 and was much more controversial. For, as an average, at one end it was far too generous for those courses where attendance amounted to one evening a week and, at the other end, it covered nothing like the costs of those degree courses which required attendance on two or three evenings a week.

The NAB Continuing Education Group recommended that the evening weighting should be increased – a simple enough proposition which hit two snags. Any general increase in the weighting would be even more generous to the one-evening-a-week courses. Moreover, with the overall funding total fixed, an increase in the weighting of evening work transferred funds from full-time work. As most evening work took place in the smaller colleges, while most full-time work took place in the polytechnics, the effect of such a funding change would be to switch funds from the polytechnics to the smaller colleges. This was the opposite of what was intended when the proposal was first advanced, for its motivation was to redress the underfunding of part-time degree work in the polytechnics. Yet, paradoxically, the outcome, if the proposal had been accepted, would have been a reduction in funds to the polytechnics; an example of the perverse impact of the use of funding incentives mentioned in the opening section. In this case, the funding mechanisms were insufficiently sophisticated to produce the necessary effect.

One way of overcoming this problem was to distinguish evening degree work from other evening work and to apply the higher weighting to the former only. Initially this came up against the bureaucratic argument that it would add another layer of complexity to what was already a very complex funding methodology. Given that the sums involved were relatively small, it was argued that the benefits were not worth the effort. Eventually, however, and not without some sustained political pressure, the NAB agreed to increase the weighting for evening degree students to 0.4.

The change certainly increased the funding to those institutions undertaking evening degree work but it is difficult to assess whether it changed behaviour. There does not seem to have been any significant increase in recruitment or in the development of new courses. On the other hand, it can be, and has been, argued that the increased funding was necessary and came just in time to prevent courses closing. For, during the early 1980s, institutions were able to subsidize their evening degree provision from the rest of their funding. But, as funding became tighter through the decade, this was no longer possible. The increased funding was needed simply to preserve the status quo.

Another example of the difficulty of targeting financial incentives is the proposal which also emerged from the NAB Continuing Education Group on providing financial support for part-time students. The theory behind such a proposal, reasonably enough, was that part-time students are relatively disadvantaged in relation to full-time students who receive fee support and maintenance grants. Equality of treatment on a pro-rata basis was proposed.

The major argument against this proposal was that many, if not most, part-time students were in employment or had spouses or partners who were in employment. They could therefore afford the generally low fees and study costs involved. To provide a general scheme of funding support would therefore, it was argued, be spending money where it was not needed.

The response to this was a proposal for a means-tested system, but here bureaucracy intervened. The complexity of such a system would mean, it was argued, that the administrative costs would be out of all proportion to the sums involved. In any event, the government has made it clear that it considers the existing system of maintenance support for full-time students to be 'too generous'. At the end of 1988 it produced a White Paper for top-up loans which clearly signalled a move in the opposite direction. The White Paper is concerned exclusively with full-time students but, if its proposals came into force and part-time students were also deemed eligible for subsidized loans, they would be in a better position than now. Moreover, with the Training Agency establishing a loans scheme for training needs, there seems no reason why such an adaptation would not be possible.

The 1985 Green Paper, while specifying that the vast bulk of the funds for continuing education should come from students and their employers, did acknowledge the need for pump-priming funds. These have been provided through PICKUP schemes in both sectors of higher education. They have been very valuable, enabling institutions to develop their capacity to provide short courses and consultancy services to private- and public-sector employers. They are, however, directed at that end rather than the access end of the continuing-education spectrum.

While central government during the 1980s has moved crab-like towards the adoption of policies favouring access, many local education authorities have embraced the policy with enthusiasm. Moreover, while central government has almost exclusively used encouragement and exhortation with little in the way of financial incentive, a number of local authorities have provided substantial finance in pursuit of the policy.

In large part this has taken the form of funding Access courses in their local further-education colleges and, in some cases, providing maintenance grants for the students who enrol. The Inner London Education Authority during the 1980s, however, also used finance to attract students in a more direct manner. It accepted that the recruitment and tuition of non-standard students imposed higher costs on its polytechnics. The higher recruitment costs were incurred through the development of close links with the further-education colleges, the involvement of polytechnic staff in joint development, delivery and evaluation of Access courses, and the time needed to interview and make individual judgements about the potential of each non-standard applicant to benefit from higher education. Higher teaching costs might also be incurred through the greater learning support and pastoral care such students often required.

To reflect these higher costs and to provide an incentive to its polytechnics actively to recruit such students, the ILEA weighted them more highly in its funding formula. It also added its own funds to those provided by the NAB so that the weighting system was not just redistribution of an existing cake but provided a clear incentive to institutions.

The five inner London polytechnics would claim that this funding system simply helped them to achieve what they were already committed to – an expansion of access, and there is much truth in this. In any event, it is about to be tested for the government's rate-capping of ILEA has meant that, since 1986, the amount it has provided over and above NAB funds fell dramatically, and by 1988 it was minimal. Additional funding to reflect non-standard entry has now disappeared in advance of the abolition of ILEA itself in 1990.

Institutional behaviour

While national policies, largely through encouragement and exhortation, have set the framework for access, the action has taken place within institutions. Moreover, the initiatives for new developments have been taken almost exclusively by institutions (or, to be more precise, small groups of staff within them). National policy has usually been a reaction to what already existed. It has rarely pioneered. 'Ability to benefit' had been a long-standing *de facto* criterion for entry used in many polytechnics and colleges before it was given *'de jure'* status by the NAB/UGC statement. New approaches to attracting non-standard entrants were already well established before the DES request to local authorities in 1978 to promote Access courses. It has been the enthusiasm and commitment of key staff, often with at best the acquiescence of their institutional leaders, which has been responsible for most developments.

This is not to minimize the role of national policy but to set it in its proper context. That role is one of facilitator of, or barrier to, developments which originate within institutions. The access developments of the 1970s in the polytechnics were facilitated by the open pooling arrangements which then existed. They were hindered by the then CNAA regulations on non-standard entrants. The continued developments in the 1980s were facilitated by the reformulation of the CNAA's regulations and its funding of development studies on various aspects of access; and by the reports of the funding bodies which raised government and public awareness, stimulated debate and encouraged those working in the field to continue. Those developments were hindered by inadequacies of funding (though not unduly), by governmental hints about concerns with quality, and by a general cultural presumption led by the universities that standard students were to be preferred if you could attract them.

The importance of institutional initiative is reflected in the many national reports which direct the bulk of their recommendations to institutions and particularly to institutional leaders. The importance of the institutional dimension can be seen by the very different behaviour of neighbouring institutions in the same urban environment and working within the same national context of policy. That policy may make it easier or harder for institutions to do what they want, but what institutions want to do is still of paramount importance.

Into the 1990s

This will become even more apparent in the 1990s. The national framework, as set out by Mr Baker's Lancaster speech, is being put into place. It is in the classic mode of a great deal of encouragement and exhortation but little by way of financial incentive. Those institutions which wish to widen access will be encouraged by the statements and will ignore the lack of financial incentive, while those who are not concerned with access will ignore the statements and profess to be discouraged by the lack of financial incentive.

In fact, demography and the financial disincentive of not being able to recruit sufficient numbers of standard students will drive many hitherto uninterested institutions down the access route. They will not need any special financial incentives or encouraging speeches from Mr Baker or his successors to be persuaded.

When the financial wolf is at the door, it is remarkable what manner of educational dogma can be cast off. So, without any help from national policies in the next few years, many institutions will suddenly discover how poor a predictor A levels are of final-degree performance; how much more interesting mature students are to teach; how easy it is to persuade women to take technological courses and how much more sense it makes to have special programmes designed to attract ethnic-minority students.

A generous government and sympathetic funding bodies, using the exhortatory and financial tools at their disposal, would make the task of widening access easier. But they are neither necessary nor sufficient conditions for access to occur. Responsive institutions are.

References

Department of Education and Science and the Scottish Education Department (1978) *Higher Education into the 1990s: A Discussion Document*, London, Department of Education and Science.

Department of Education and Science (1979) *Future Trends in Higher Education*, London, Department of Education and Science.

Department of Education and Science (1985) *The Development of Higher Education into the 1990s*, Cmnd 9524, London, HMSO.

Lucas, S. and Ward, P. (1985) *A Survey of Access Courses in England*, Lancaster, University of Lancaster.

National Advisory Body (1984a) *Report of Continuing Education Group*, London, NAB.

National Advisory Body (1984b) *A Strategy for Higher Education in the late 1980s and Beyond*, London, NAB.

University Grants Committee (1984a) *Report of the Continuing Education Working Party*, London, HMSO.

University Grants Committee (1984b) *A Strategy for Higher Education into the 1990s*, London, HMSO.

Woodley, A., Wagner, L., Slowey, M., Hamilton, M. and Fulton, O. (1987)
Choosing to Learn: Adults in Education, Milton Keynes, SRHE and Open
University Press.

10

Creating the Accessible Institution

Chris Duke

What is 'the accessible institution'?

The term 'access', while fashionable, is problematic in several ways. On the face of it 'institution', here meaning simply an institution of higher education (HE), should present less difficulty. (There is the particular difficulty that the arrival of 'autonomy' and the Polytechnics and Colleges Funding Council (PCFC) in the so-called public sector make for even more uncertainty there. This reinforces my instinct to write mainly of the university sector with which I am more familiar.) However, Part 1 of this volume, in addressing 'boundaries and partnerships', immediately suggests that here too things may be less simple than they seem.

This section seeks to address what is problematic about each of these terms. It also touches upon several aspects of institutional life important to the process of fostering change from within. The purpose behind the chapter is to examine ways in which those who play a part in managing higher-education institutions in the Britain of the nineties may work for desirable change. In what ways is institutional proactivity possible? Does it make sense in these times to write about creating institutions from within? Or is it more a matter of refashioning by external forces to which the managers of institutions react, always too late and always on the defensive?

In the previous chapter Leslie Wagner gave his optimistic answer from the perspective of an institutional leader reacting to external pressures and constraints. Can the analysis of internal processes lead us to a similar conclusion?

Accessible

Of 'accessible' we might ask in what senses, to whom, and for what purposes. The hard core of the access debate concerns participation by different socio-economic groups in higher education: the continuing domination by middle-class students of eighteen-plus entry; falling cohort sizes at this age for the immediate planning period; and the readiness or otherwise of HE institutions to recognize and welcome bearers of new, and less traditional, less academic, forms of qualification as evidence of suitability for HE (TVEI, GCSE, AS levels, vocationally oriented qualifications taken in school or further-education college, even, as through YTS, partly in the workplace). The waters here are further muddied by speculation about financial support both for individuals and for institutions (loans, vouchers, Australian-style repayment through the income-tax system, fee variation, even 'opting out'); by uncertainty as to how far traditionally excluded groups and categories might respond to Lord Chilver's call to aspiring university students to 'prove their commitment by being prepared to find the full cost themselves' (*Times Higher Education Supplement*, 14 October 1988); and how far Mr Baker's preference for an American over a European road to mass higher education, declared at Lancaster in January 1989, will be taken. Around this core, but closely connected if only by the falling cohort sizes of school-leaving age, is 'capital-A Access', as it is commonly called by those concerned with Access courses designed to bring older students into higher education, usually via the further-education (FE) system, but increasingly now also by HE institutions themselves. The 'capital-A' distinguishes this relatively formalized access provision from the wider issues of institutional accessibility enabling adults to get back into and move in and out through the lattice-work of FE/HE provision at their own pace, in their chosen sequence, to meet their different particular circumstances and needs. Whereas the 'hard core' and 'capital-A Access' are concerned essentially with finding places on award-bearing (usually degree) courses – and increasingly also with curriculum change to make such courses more attractive to non-traditional students – the 'access movement', characterized, for instance, by the Forum for Access Studies (FAST) and the proliferating access federations around the country, is concerned, as earlier chapters in this book have shown, with wider considerations, both practical and philosophical, to do with what HE institutions are, how they deliver, and how they feel to those not enrolled as traditional, regular, students.

All of this concerns access to award-bearing courses: to the mainstream of what it is traditionally understood higher-education teaching is about. Widening access means drawing into this award-bearing system excluded groups and categories: young people of working-class background and older participants from all socio-economic groups, with a particular eye to those marginalized in terms of class, gender and race. It means access not just to the learning opportunities offered by HE but also to the extrinsic rewards: qualifications having recognized currency especially in the job market. The distinction is well illustrated by the British university extramural tradition. Historically it has displayed considerable ambivalence over certification of study (Duke and Marriott 1974). Recently there has been expansion from extramural certification into the award-bearing areas of Access courses and part-time degrees. In the hitherto marginalized extramural world, where 'mainstreaming' of continuing education (CE) has become a strategic priority, access has come to refer to the *qualifications* offered by universities rather than, mainly or exclusively, university-level educational opportunity. The term 'extramural' is also going out of fashion and use. However 'outreach', 'distance', and 'open learning' retain or are gaining in favour; all are in principle modes for enhancing access to educational institutions and provision in non-traditional ways. (The term 'external', now adopted by the old extramural department at Leeds as well as by Oxford, adds to the linguistic ambiguities to do with the idea of the accessible institution; no longer is 'external' restricted, in the London and Australian sense, to an 'internal' degree taken externally.)

Before we turn to the ambiguities concerning 'institution', let us ask again 'to whom and for what?' Parts of some universities and colleges belong quite fully to the community in terms of use: the sports facilities and the Arts Centre at Warwick for example. The local civic fathers and shire councillors may feel that it is 'their polytechnic', 'their university'. The feeling may increasingly be shared by local captains of industry who come to identify with, support and influence the local polytechnic or university, as did their forebears when the nineteenth-century redbricks were founded. In return for financial and other support they may have access to (and indeed share in or dominate the creation of) consultancy, research and development, and continuing-education short courses tailored to their particular needs. The sense of access may not be shared equally by other local stakeholders in the British commonweal. Or it may be felt mainly in respect of the sporting and cultural aspects of the institution furthest from the institutional heartland, and incidentally in terms of non-award study allowing but peripheral contact with the main business of the institution.

Institution

Of 'institution' we might ask how firm and static a phenomenon this is. It may be conceived as a monolith (conventionally an ivory tower), access to which is by a narrow and well-protected route with entry hurdles (and maybe an extramural off-licence round the back). Or we may look at polytechnics, colleges and universities as they now actually are, including their rate and direction of change. The 'membership' of a university, if once it was clear cut, is now ambiguous in a sociological and even a contractual sense. If we leave aside assumptions about the 'academic community' as distinct from the whole socio-technical system, the complete payroll, who enjoys membership of the institution in any real sense? Some may technically be members, whether students, cleaners or lecturers, yet feel dissociated and alienated. Others may have a casual, honorary or

part-time affiliation as teachers or fellows, yet identify strongly with the
institution (or with a department or group) and feel very much a part of it.
Full-time students taking degrees may be a minority of those who are
registered with the nominal designation of a student at the institution –
though a larger proportion of the output as measured in full-time
equivalents after allowing for the divisors applied to part-time study in its
various forms (see Chapter 9). Performance measures and reward systems
trail reality in respect of the total teaching–learning effort of an HE
institution.

Membership in terms of intellectual and related productive effort, by
way of consultancy, research and development, teaching companies and
other industrial and community partnerships, is wider still. On the
academic staff side there are changes of tenure and trends towards
short-term, fractional, pump-primed and contract-funded appointments,
bought-in and maybe increasingly contracted-out teaching. All of these,
together with expansion of sandwich and other industrial partnerships,
modularization, accumulation and transfer of credit, recognition of prior
learning and in-company education and training towards the institution's
awards, mean that HE institutions are coming to lack sharply defined
membership and boundaries. We are moving away from a separate guild or
community of scholars. Keeping term and counting the nights towards
one's degree appears yet more anachronistic than it did to the Oxbridge
scholar of the sixties. If the Universities Funding Council (UFC) goes the
way Lord Chilver's and indeed Mr Baker's thoughts suggest, earning and
learning will be combined for increasing numbers of young as well as older
people. Thus the distinct student (especially undergraduate) role as well as
the distinct adult student role will increasingly blur and dissolve, along with
the boundaries of higher-education institutions.

As the boundaries of HE institutions become increasingly permeable, we
see, as part of the process, the introjection of outside forces and influences:
not only at the level of governing bodies but in working as well as advisory
senses at all levels through the institution. Collaboration and partnership,
often sponsored by government departments and programmes via local
collaborative projects, consortia, regional technology centres and so forth,
imply a more distant, negotiated, form of co-operation than the introjection and interpenetration suggested here. Short of mergers in the full
sense, but going well beyond regional networks and partnerships, the
institutions' boundaries, distinct identities and missions, seem to be
blurring and melding faster than any policy or legislation dictates. The
FHE system, embedded within its different industrial (or economic) and
broader 'communities' and bombarded with policy interventions from
central government has broken up the tidy UFC–PCFC FE–HE model and
presents quite another picture. Those in HE are coming to create new
definitions of reality, new ideologies of HE, new legitimations for what they
do to survive. The polytechnics find this on the whole easier because their
traditions and missions are closer to this new reality than to the ideal of the

residential Oxbridge community of scholars. Even here, however, before asking how to create the (more) accessible institution, we must ask what an 'HE institution' already is and is likely to be. What in this sense will be the Open Polytechnic; or, internationally, the Commonwealth of Learning? How are these to be distinguished from their 'partner-members'? Can we encircle on the map of activity and say: 'What happens inside this is the college (or university) of X; beyond it are other things'?

The process of creating more access

'We think the way we hunt moose. Never in a straight line because then the moose knows where you are. You go around and around the moose, coming closer all the time until you finally close in on him' (Denis and Richter 1987: 25). One would like to be able to set out in tidy and logical sequence the steps whereby HE institutions can and maybe do proceed to create wider access – especially since this chapter makes the optimistic and purposeful assumption that institutions should and can choose and set new directions, and not be entirely subject to external policies and market forces. In fact the process might be more like the non-linear moose-hunting techniques which Denis and Richter cite as an approach to intuitive learning. Denis identified 18 processes, but no logical or linear sequence between them. There may be prerequisites for an institution to promote enhanced access successfully, but no one best means of pursuing this objective. Partly this is because each institution is in some respects unique, often consciously and proudly so. Partly it is because managed change, social engineering, is such an imprecise art. This implies a set of possible interventions or initiatives within the ongoing life of the institution, each of which will tend directly to enhance or indirectly to facilitate access. The internal condition of the institution as well as its environment may be more or less receptive to such change, perhaps on a normal curve of distribution rather than simply a long spectrum. That is to say, too much or too little threat, too much or too little institutional self-confidence, may equally hinder innovation – an important tactical point for governments to bear in mind in pressing change upon universities. The implication of this is that the process of creating more access is a matter of creating and sustaining a sense of direction, and of exploiting and connecting up opportunities as they present themselves, rather than prescribing and following set rules for moving from A to B: more like the way battles are actually fought than the way commanders would have one believe they manage them.

There is more to this than opportunism, handy ingredient as that is. It implies a sense of vision; the capacity to create and promote an alternative yet favourable scenario for the future; ability to understand and reassure principled and concerned opponents of change: skills of leadership as well as horse-trading. In the access arena it requires a capacity to see the connections between different, superficially discrete, incidents, initiatives and opportunities, and to draw them together as an interactive, maybe integrative, system of change: to create and enhance synergy. In a moment we will proceed to list a number of these initiatives, and to consider, non-prescriptively, the possible interactions between them, and the conditions which may be necessary to an effective access-creating process.

Before that a more personal note, partly of self-denial. For a continuing educator who has in recent times seen his guild of tradesfolk invited in from the stables to the chancellorial halls, it is tempting to dwell almost exclusively on the role of CE as catalyst and change agent, pointer and pathway to the future. CE indisputably represents an important way of enhancing access to HE, and bringing the goods and services of HE to new groups and sectors – community down-market as well as industrial up-market where the will is there to do both. It also provides a potent means for trying out new things in a more protected, lower-risk way which, if satisfying and satisfactory, may then be imported into the regular mainstream work of university – into its knowledge-creating as well as its knowledge-transmitting activities. CE is thus both a form of access and a means of innovation which can extend access within pre-experience education, research and consultancy. It is however still more commonly bolted on than embedded (in current PICKUP parlance), and therefore quite easily unbolted if this proves expedient. One measure of an accessible institution is how widely and freely its most precious wares are available. This means above all the degrees for which it is renowned, the teaching and other resources which support these, and the enhanced life opportunities which they represent for those gaining entry. CE, therefore, is treated here as but one thread in the bundle of activities and policy initiatives which, woven together, can indeed create a more accessible institution.

Access initiatives and opportunities include the following:

- provision of Access courses by the HE institution allowing non-standard entry adults admission to degree courses (of one's own and/or other HE institutions).
- provision of foundation-year-type closed- or link-Access courses into particular degree courses (e.g. in engineering) whereby successful completion of the foundation course allows automatic progression to the regular degree.
- recognition (or validation) of Access courses in other institutions, usually neighbouring colleges of further education, allowing serious, or equal, or specially favoured, consideration of the (non-traditional) students on such courses for entry to degree courses (such as guarantee of an interview).
- favourable and flexible consideration of candidates applying from Access courses elsewhere for admission to degree courses, as part of an open attitude to non-standard entry generally.
- the practice of openness and flexibility towards all candidates seeking entry to degree courses without normal entry qualifications, including

willingness to recognize prior, experiential and other non-academic learning, to devise appropriate means of considering particular individuals' potential, etc.

- willingness to acknowledge, accept and take risks with new forms of qualification among young applicants coming out of new school assessment systems and through non-academic (FE, YTS, ET) routes.
- acceptance of some measures and forms of affirmative action and monitoring in respect of groups with low levels of participation in HE, particularly minority ethnic groups and, in some subjects, women.
- recognition of professional, occupational and academic attainment in other institutions and enterprises, with a view to giving advanced standing in appropriate courses.
- acceptance and practice of credit accumulation and transfer more generally, and by means of specific and deliberate arrangements where geographical and other factors suggest a special case.
- creation of intermediate awards for those who are unable to complete a full (honours) degree but have not failed in what they have had time and resources to attempt (certificate-diploma-degree structure).
- creation of new routes into and through curricula and programmes of study to make them more accessible in practice to those whose circumstances prevent them following the traditional three-year full-time honours route, by such means as:

  - modularization of degree courses and parts thereof (to different sizes and linkages of units for different purposes).
  - rescheduling of teaching times during the working day, week and year to create opportunities for face-to-face teaching–learning for different groups (housewives, shift-workers and other occupational and social groups).
  - ensuring that teaching and learning venues are accessible to the physically handicapped, and child-care facilities available for those with young children.
  - creation of part-time degree programmes allowing day, evening and mixed time study.
  - use of study centres, outreach or open-learning centres for those for whom the campus is too inaccessible, and appropriate mixes of mode, e.g. to include short residential periods on campus.
  - partnership with other providers (HE, OU, FE, industry, community agencies) to make university study available through collaborative provision, including 'franchising', validation and other forms of partnership.
  - consideration of new routes and steps into regular and new degree programmes via extramural and other continuing-education courses.
  - review of degree programmes, both whole degrees and course by course, including entry prerequisites, to ensure that unnecessary

obstacles are not being perpetuated and that curricula have not become unnecessarily encumbered through accretion of new with old material.

This list, though long enough, is by no means complete. To take just one example, developments since 1979 by the tiny Extra-Mural Studies Office at Lancaster include (following participation in the Open College of the North-West): Open Lectures (1980); a Mature Students' Study Skills Programme (1980); the Summer Programme, Town-Centre Lectures and Part 1 Part-time Degree Study (1981); University of the Third Age and Part 2 Part-time Degree Study (1982); an Unemployed Adults' Programme (1983); Occasional Students (1986); and Community Learners (1987). This work, which by no means comprises a full inventory of that university's access activities, is complemented by empirical research by the Office into the education of adults (Percy 1988: 109).

The list is also perhaps obvious – as are the links between the different elements. One can quickly see how successful innovation in one or two of these areas may ease the way for other changes similarly designed to improve access for non-traditional students who are proving a pleasure to teach and have around – if only because familiarity can breed a measure of confidence in new kinds of students and programmes. Some other possible changes may be more controversial, or more problematic in resource terms. Not everyone would see the university having a responsibility for assessing prior learning gained in the factory, home or community, or validating courses conducted by and in other institutions, except where there is a direct link with or prospect of recruitment to that university. Provision of bursary funds from within the university's own resources might be thought desirable in principle but financially impracticable; or even undesirable in principle, as removing a responsibility that resides with the State.

Another set of possible changes is less obviously, less directly, connected to creating access, yet may be no less important. In addition there are still less tangible considerations of leadership style and organization culture to take into the reckoning. Associated with these, creating the accessible institution may imply changes of character so fundamental that they cannot be achieved by consensus, leaving the options of not changing (and maybe thereby contracting and even dying); or of changing by *force majeure*; or of change by manipulation and accretion without being explicit about purposes and intended outcomes. Each of these options carries attendant risks. Consideration and rejection of a major change enhancing access at Aberdeen makes interesting reading through such lenses.

An example of the important indirect factors is criteria for promotion of academic staff. It remains received wisdom in 1989 that promotion depends on academic publications first, second and third, with a possible makeweight of teaching ability, contribution to administration and university life, and community service. Research income, it is thought, may now be nudging in with the dominant measure of research output. In fact many universities do now give prominence to criteria other than research, and anecdotal evidence suggests that some take these sufficiently seriously to base decisions on them, by no means the same thing. However, so long as the perception, or myth, survives to the contrary, it operates as a fact: as a factor in dissuading academic staff from investing in time-consuming curriculum development, innovation in teaching forms and methods, short-course and access-course activity, or community-relations work of different kinds which may create access to university expertise and resources via consultancy and research and development but is unlikely to yield refereed publications. Thus creating the accessible institution implies changing not only promotion criteria but promotion outcomes and, equally, the perception and recognition of these.

Organizational culture and leadership style permeate the institution and largely determine its experienced character, both for the members within its increasingly uncertain boundaries, and for those who seek access to it as outsiders. They are discovered by the latter less commonly by meeting the vice-chancellor than by being welcomed or rebuffed by switchboard operators and porters. The personality and style of the vice-chancellor can, however, quite quickly influence the character of the institution as experienced by the casual visitor or the anxious inquirer. Is access, accessibility, modelled from the top – in the conduct of business, the presentation of financial data, the sharing of strategic and business planning? What priorities and values are demonstrated by the way the leader's time is spent, meetings are conducted, annual reports phrased and ordered? What does the attitude to staff development, industrial second-ments and community partnerships, even the handling of day-to-day public relations, say about the institution's valuing of 'access'?

Does the institution have an explicit mission statement, and if so is it known and 'owned' by all the members? A colleague's recent visit to Salford was reported to be memorable, especially for the fact that porters and technicians as well as department heads knew the Salford mission statement, could pull it from their pockets and cite their part and contribution. Maybe such a formal document is culturally alien to the special style and history of many British institutions. None the less, they may have, or lack, a sense of vision, purpose and integrity which is widely shared and widely valued; and which is favourable, or inimical, to access. It will be reflected in the style and efficiency of committee work and decision-making (or -ducking); and in the sense of optimism, pride and buoyancy (or conversely low or shattered morale) felt around the place.

A question arises here. Since universities in particular (in contrast to colleges and polytechnics which have different traditions and management systems) are more like loose federations of baronies (engineering, classics?) and/or tribes (social sciences?), not to mention the apotheosis of individual-ism in the name of academic autonomy, does it make any sense to write of mission statements and the organization? Is it possible for a good academic to be a 'good company man'? Or is loyalty only to the discipline, and to the department within which it is guarded? The trend towards cost centres, the periodic talk of business schools opting out and going private, may point in this direction. On the other hand, many of the pressures affecting higher education – for mass higher education, for a more market-driven, consumer-responsive approach, for diversified income sources and re-duced public expenditure – and the need to win back public and political esteem, tend to press institutions to create a stronger corporate identity and public image: witness the preoccupation with names and logos of late. The message is that the college of X or the university of Y is an open, user-friendly, useful resource to the locality and region as well as a national resource of international stature. I doubt if the reader could find a single British HE institution where even a cursory examination did not reveal (a) several examples of the press for favourable and public corporate identity and (b) a strong element of community service (in one form or another) within this. That being so, what we are witnessing is an already existing phenomenon of the whole HE system, through all its members, jostling for an access identity. Widely differing levels of intelligence and competence are displayed in the protracted and complex task of moving these (basically conservative) institutions around within a (basically conservative) system in a (basically conservative) society. A prerequisite to even moderate success however, a necessary though not sufficient condition, is strong, preferably open, leadership, a sense of mission (or values and direction), capacity to effect and implement reasonably rapid decisions, and the ability to discern and make connections between nominally separate, piecemeal changes. Whether and how these conditions are met will vary with each unique institution of HE, presumably with still greater diversity in the university than in the 'public' sector.

An illustrative example

The history of the University of Warwick has been brief but eventful. A mid-1960s foundation, it is now the largest of the green-fields universities, with the advantage, at any rate from an access perspective, that, while its campus enjoys the green and leafy character for which Warwickshire is renowned, land was also donated by the City of Coventry whose housing estates it adjoins. Alongside it has grown up the thriving Science Park, and on an adjacent site now is springing up Coventry's Business Park. To some Coventry residents the University still feels psychologically remote and a long way away, although it is but three miles to the centre of this large, compact, industrial city. Ironically, while some polytechnics seek green(er) fields away from London, an aid to access for some sixties foundations might be to move in the opposite direction.

Warwick's first Vice-Chancellor now sits on the government benches as a life peer – a reminder not to discuss access in a tritely political way, recognizing too that R. H. Tawney is a spiritual forebear of the access movement. Butterworth created a vigorous and expansionist university which scored high on access on several dimensions, although its own first Access course in that specific sense was started only in 1987. Before then good Access links had been created with several nearby colleges, and a University-led open-learning federation was already informally in being.

Warwick's early tumultuous years did not bode well, nor would 'access' have sprung to mind as an obvious descriptor in the early seventies. None the less the close links with industry created then, when private sector funding was less fashionable than today, and the Arts Centre which has grown to become the largest such cultural centre outside the Barbican, each manifest the orientation towards community relations, partnerships and service in one form or another which distinguish Warwick today. They laid the base, in terms of institutional culture as well as direct experience of 'community' openness and collaboration, of permeable boundaries and interpenetration with other influences and institutions, for the explicit access policies and programmes of more recent years. Warwick practised late-1980s behaviour well before this was thrust on the whole HE system by government. Consequently, as Martin Trow, the Californian scholar of higher education, has observed, it suffered 'seven lean years' in the wilderness before coming into the good years. In recent years Warwick has enjoyed high esteem and relatively favourable public funding, with expansion in many areas at the same time as, and partly as a result of, ranking very high in the league table for non-UGC as a proportion of total income. Its second Vice-Chancellor brought with him personal experience of the advantages of 'access' (post-experience and recurrent education, credit transfer) as well as professional knowledge of the much more open US, and specifically the Californian, system. The institutional culture favouring access was thus further strengthened, and at the same time deliberately extended into the (more down-market) forms and areas which tend most readily to spring to mind when the term access is employed.

The method employed to promote access more deliberately and explicitly was the creation, after some unavoidable delay, in 1985 of a Department of Continuing Education enjoying academic stature and conditions within one of the four faculties (Educational Studies), but with a very particular and, for Britain, novel brief. Warwick was built on a tradition of appointing strong departmental leaders and giving them their heads: a system which produces close links between departments and centre, a weak intermediary level, and the capacity (so long presumably as a certain but unknown size is not exceeded?) for open communication, sharing of culture and purpose, and very rapid decision-making. In this context a regular academic department was chosen as the means, but the brief was broadly encompassing and institution wide: effectively to promote continuing education in the widest sense and in its many forms throughout the University, and in collaboration with other institutions and agencies in the region. The founding Chairman was also appointed

University Director of Open Studies and an ex-officio member of Senate (as well as of the General Entrance Requirement Committee), and Co-ordinator of the (existing) Coventry Consortium – a University-led PICKUP consortium of FE and HE institutions, the first of its kind in the country. Waiting on the table were a commitment in principle to start a new system of part-time first degrees (a commitment made in the late seventies but without what in Warwick is called a champion available to take up the cause) and requests for help or support from various local FE colleges to start or develop further provision and recognition of access courses.

The Department was not made a distinct cost centre. It was not drawn in with other income-generating units under the rubric of the (significant and successful) Earned Income Group (EIG). Instead it was resourced on exactly the same basis and terms as other academic departments and areas: through the annual cycle of bidding, appealing, and accounting to the Estimates and Grants Committee (EGC). It must be added that it has been very well supported and favourably treated by that key committee of Senate in the annual competition for scarce resources – a manifestation of the institutional culture and commitment to the access and continuing education mission of the University, for which the Department is one important means. Thus the curious duality and tension – competing academic department and yet central catalyst and facility – have been quite remarkably easily sustained. Although the Department is a direct provider of courses via the Open Studies Programme (liberal adult education in old and new forms together with a range of seminars, courses and workshops mainly in the professional CE area) it is not in competition with other departments. Its role is to suggest, foster and assist the development of CE and access (in all the diverse forms) throughout the institution. The University already had major programmes of continuing education, especially in Manufacturing Systems and Business Studies. The new Department assists further development in these areas, occasionally acting as a formal partner in development and provision, and works to extend such activity into other parts of the University. Briefly, this has tended to mean: extending post-experience vocational education (PEVE) activity – PICKUP and others – into areas where there is (more or less obvious) potential for some kind of vocational updating; creating and expanding a new system of part-time degrees, initially in the less vocationally oriented departments in Arts and Social Studies (roughly speaking, the other half of the University); and acting within and on behalf of the University to explore and promote a range of other developments, each having to do with enhanced access and community relations. These include: the promotion of credit accumulation and transfer, for instance by means of informal co-operation and a formal agreement with the CNAA Credit Accumulation and Transfer Scheme; regional collaboration in the area of staff development, both for CE/PEVE and more generally; partnerships with such diverse local bodies as the Anglican Diocese, the local education authorities in the region, other educational institutions, public- and private-sector organizations, voluntary, community and interest groups (e.g. in natural and local history, for archaeological and environmental studies), and the various parties with a stake in the problems and future in Inner City Coventry. In the last case the University, through the CE Department, is seeking to create a physical and human presence in this deprived and partly ghettoized area, in order to make its resources more practically accessible to the groups and individuals in that area. At the same time it has brought into being the Forum for Access to Midlands Education, a regional access federation within which ideas and courses can be developed, recognized and reviewed, and staff development and support provided. At the kernel of this is located the Joint Recognition and Review Committee (JRRC) of the University and Coventry Polytechnic, which systematizes and facilitates access work in the region in partnership with the FE colleges, which are represented on the JRRC. University commitment to Access is thus on a basis of regional collaboration and mainly by supporting the work of others rather than making direct provision. Where a particular role for the University becomes apparent, such as innovation, action research and development, then direct provision will be considered. A new-format two-year course for Priority Area residents is offered jointly with Coventry (Community Education Programme), and a new version of this, as a three-way partnership with the Polytechnic, is being discussed.

It would be indulgent to multiply examples of access initiatives, and misleading to suggest that all are equally and easily successful. The decision to introduce part-time degrees was closely contested. Central objections could be refuted only by taking the plunge and testing the doubts through experience: demand, quality and standards, administration, and so forth. Nor is there then a resting place. New cohorts create new levels of administrative complexity; extending into new subject areas means rehearsing all the arguments and offering assurances all over again. Meanwhile the £50,000 voted by University Council to develop the work in the absence of UGC funding is gradually spent, along with a bursary fund generously created by four strong departments to meet the fees of needy students, fully or in part, so that more internal subvention looks necessary around the corner. Similarly with mature-age students coming from Access courses, one department appears not to understand at all what it is all about; yet the Law School, like many other departments heavily oversubscribed with high A-level achievers and unable to contribute to the part-time degrees, makes space for black Access students as a matter of principle. One seminar-cum-briefing session for Admissions Tutors packs the Council Chamber; another attracts but a handful.

The case for many of these developments is made, and sustained, by a somewhat general but apparently powerful appeal to the shared belief in Warwick: as a buoyant, bustling, innovative and entrepreneurial – yet caring – institution. People will try many things partly because they are new, out of pride that Warwick does lead with many kinds of innovation. Behind this (rather than very obviously above it) is the known support of key leaders and opinion-makers in the University. Both leadership and institutional culture thus favour creating a more accessible institution. This is seen as advancing, not jeopardizing, the institutional interest (Warwick might be described as a selfish and therefore a successful and relatively accessible university); and access initiatives, like any others, are welcome as initiatives but subjected to the same generally efficient and hard-nosed scrutiny as any others. Making the institution more accessible, then, is hard work, but rewarding because the necessary conditions are present and can be exploited.

Implications

Let us ask, by way of conclusion, whether it is indeed both worth while and feasible to create significantly more accessible institutions. My stress is on the act of creation by the membership and leadership of institutions. For there can be little doubt that higher education *will* become much more accessible over the next decade, by whatever means and at whatever cost to character, quality and morale, through external direction or manipulation, if institutions do not change themselves.

More positively, however, the implication of this chapter is that enhanced access can be created from within, and that it is eminently worth while to do this. A national-interest perspective dictates that HE moves towards what is commonly called mass (and away from élite) provision, probably with some further measure of diversification between institutions, but with few if any exempt from this access shift. The evidence so far is that, while demography may threaten standards in certain subjects and certain institutions, in terms of 18-plus entry scores, increasing the access and numbers of non-traditional students has without exception enhanced the quality of work, and life, in higher education. The low retention rate of post-16 schooling in Britain suggests that there is much room for expanding especially mature-age intake without any need to lower standards.

On the other hand, the accessible institution will not be the same place as the institution out of which it grew. There is widespread agreement (excepting perhaps a significant proportion of university scholar-specialists from this) that the English single-honours first degree, though of a very high standard and very successful apropos wastage within its own terms, is not well fashioned to meet the needs of late twentieth-century society and its members. The cultural shift within leading institutions will have to become a national culture shift before the implications of expanding participation rates (and so widening both 18-plus and adult access) are absorbed and adopted throughout the larger educational enterprise. HE institutions will be still more different places than present changes – new forms of governance for polytechnics and colleges, partial 'privatization' and 'marketization' of institutional character and effort – indicate. The boundaries and membership of HE institutions will become much more blurred – even in those cases where single campuses on distinct sites survive. The paradigm shift in HE is under way, but the new paradigm is not yet clearly formed, much less accepted. The central value, however, of opportunity open to the talents, of a more effective blend of excellence with equity, of vigorous scholarly effort with realistic efficiency, accountability and – even – 'relevance', is worth creating, both in the mind and through institutional evolution.

   Seen thus, the access debate is a debate about the future, and the soul, of the university. It is also unavoidably a debate about the identity and future of the nation, as the *THES* suggested recently in singing 'Provincial praises'. 'How can we open up higher education if the enterprise is still seen as a means of escape from the common condition, as an initiation into a wider élite, however diffuse that notion has become in the late 1980s, as a process from which the majority must be excluded to ensure its purity. Perhaps if higher education in Britain is ever to be provided on the scale of other advanced nations it will have to become more provincial again' (*Times Higher Education Supplement*, 30 December 1988). As these 'notes from the trenches' of a modern, thoroughly provincial, university with an enviable international reputation for scholarship and research suggest, creating accessible institutions may be hard work but it is a thoroughly worthwhile and believable form of activity.

References

Abrahamsson, K., Rubenson, K. and Slowey, M. (eds) (1988) *Adults in the Academy: International Trends in Adult and Higher Education*, Stockholm, Swedish National Board of Education.

Denis, M. and Richter, I. (1987) 'Learning about intuitive learning: moose-hunting techniques', in Boud, D. and Griffin, V. (eds) *Appreciating Adult Learning: From the Learners' Perspective*, London, Kogan Page.

Duke, C. (1988) *The Future Shape of Continuing Education and Universities*, Warwick, DCE, University of Warwick.

Duke, C. and Marriott, S. (1974) *Paper Awards in Liberal Adult Education*, London, Michael Joseph.

Percy, K. (1988) 'Opening access to a modern university', in Eggins, H. (ed.) *Restructuring Higher Education*, Milton Keynes, SRHE/Open University Press.

The Times Higher Education Supplement, 14 October 1988, 30 December 1988.

Trow, M. (1988) 'Continuing education – an analysis of market forces and latent functions', in Abrahamsson *et al.* (1988).

The Society for Research into Higher Education

The Society exists both to encourage and co-ordinate research and development into all aspects of higher education, including academic, organizational and policy issues; and also to provide a forum for debate – verbal and printed.

The Society's income derives from subscriptions, book sales, conference fees, and grants. It receives no subsidies and is wholly independent. Its corporate members are institutions of higher education, research institutions and professional, industrial, and governmental bodies. Its individual members include teachers and researchers, administrators and students. Members are found in all parts of the world and the Society regards its international work as amongst its most important activities.

The Society discusses and comments on policy, organizes conferences, and encourages research. Under the imprint SRHE & OPEN UNIVERSITY PRESS, it is a specialist publisher of research, having some 40 titles in print. It also publishes *Studies in Higher Education* (three times a year), which is mainly concerned with academic issues; *Higher Education Quarterly* (formerly *Universities Quarterly*) mainly concerned with policy issues; *Abstracts* (three times a year); an *International Newsletter* (twice a year) and *SRHE News* (four times a year).

The Society's committees, study groups and branches are run by members (with help from a small secretariat at Guildford), and aim to provide a forum for discussion. The groups at present include a Teacher Education Study Group, a Staff Development Group, and a Continuing Education Group, each of which may have their own organization, subscriptions, or publications (e.g. the *Staff Development Newsletter*). A further Questions of Quality Group has organized a series of Anglo-American seminars in the USA and the UK.

The Governing Council, elected by members, comments on current issues; and discusses policies with leading figures, notably at its evening forums. The Society organizes seminars on current research, and is in touch with bodies in the UK such as the NAB, CVCP, UGC, CNAA and with sister-bodies overseas. It co-operates with the British Council on courses run in conjunction with its conferences.

The Society's conferences are often held jointly; and have considered 'Standards and Criteria' (1986, with Bulmershe College); 'Restructuring' (1987, with the City of Birmingham Polytechnic); 'Academic Freedom' (1988, with the University of Surrey). In 1989, 'Access and Institutional Change' (with the Polytechnic of North London). In 1990, the topic will be 'Industry and Higher Education' (with the University of Surrey). In 1991, the topic will be 'Research in HE'. Other conferences have considered the DES Green Paper (1985); 'HE After the Election' (1987) and 'After the Reform Act' (July 1988). An annual series on 'The First Year Experience' with the University of South Carolina and Teeside Polytechnic held two meetings in 1988 in Cambridge, and another in St Andrews in July 1989.

For some of the Society's conferences, special studies are commissioned in advance, as *Precedings*.

Members receive free of charge the Society's *Abstracts*, annual conference proceedings (or 'Precedings'), *SRHE News* and *International Newsletter*. They may buy *SRHE & Open University Press* books at discount, and *Higher Education Quarterly* on special terms. Corporate members also receive the Society's journal *Studies in Higher Education* free (individuals on special terms). Members may also obtain certain other journals at a discount, including the NFER *Register of Educational Research*. There is a substantial discount to members, and to staff of corporate members, on annual and some other conference fees.